Classroom Management from the Ground Up

Classroom management can make or break your teaching. But as educators know, there is no one-fits-all solution for every classroom. That is why bestselling authors Todd Whitaker, Madeline Whitaker Good, and Katherine Whitaker came together to write this book. They created a guide combining sound research with practical wisdom so educators could have a classroom management resource written by teachers for teachers. From this book, you'll gain effective strategies for designing and improving your classroom management from the ground up. You'll learn how the three core aspects of classroom management (relationships, high and clear expectations, and consistency) can be used to build and maintain an effectively run classroom. You'll also find out how to tweak minor issues and reset major challenges when things don't go as planned.

Each chapter covers a core aspect of classroom management and includes a foundational understanding of the concept, powerful stories and examples, how-to applications, and tips on tweaking as problems arise. In addition, each chapter features a "What You Can Do Tomorrow" section—strategies you can implement immediately. Whether you are a new or an experienced teacher, this book will empower you to identify what is going well, adjust what needs to be changed, and feel more prepared for the unexpected.

Todd Whitaker (@ToddWhitaker) is a professor of educational leadership at the University of Missouri. He is a leading presenter in the field of education and has written more than 50 books, including the national bestsellers, *What Great Teachers Do Differently* and *Your First Year: How to Survive and Thrive as a New Teacher*, co-written with Madeline Whitaker Good and Katherine Whitaker.

Madeline Whitaker Good (@MWhitakerGood) is a national presenter, author, former elementary teacher, and current middle school teacher in Springfield, Missouri.

Katherine Whitaker (@MissWhitaker294) is a national presenter, author, former middle school teacher, and current high school teacher in Kansas City, Missouri.

Other Eye On Education Books Available from Routledge

(www.routlege.com/eyeoneducation)

Your First Year: How to Survive and Thrive as a New Teacher
Todd Whitaker, Madeline Whitaker Good, and Katherine Whitaker

Dealing with Difficult Parents, 2nd Edition
Todd Whitaker and Douglas J. Fiore

A School Leader's Guide to Dealing with Difficult Parents
Todd Whitaker and Douglas J. Fiore

Study Guide to Dealing with Difficult Parents
Todd Whitaker and Douglas J. Fiore

Dealing with Difficult Teachers, 3rd Edition
Todd Whitaker

**What Great Teachers Do Differently, 2nd Edition:
17 Things That Matter Most**
Todd Whitaker

**What Great Principals Do Differently, 2nd Edition:
18 Things That Matter Most**
Todd Whitaker

What Connected Educators Do Differently
Todd Whitaker, Jeffrey Zoul, and Jimmy Casas

**Motivating & Inspiring Teachers, 2nd Edition:
The Educational Leader's Guide for Building Staff Morale**
Todd Whitaker, Beth Whitaker, and Dale Lumpa

**Teaching Matters, 2nd Edition:
How to Keep Your Passion and Thrive in Today's Classroom**
Todd Whitaker and Beth Whitaker

Great Quotes for Great Educators
Todd Whitaker and Dale Lumpa

Classroom Management from the Ground Up

Todd Whitaker, Madeline Whitaker Good,
and Katherine Whitaker

Routledge
Taylor & Francis Group

NEW YORK AND LONDON

First published 2019
by Routledge
52 Vanderbilt Avenue, New York, NY 10017

and by Routledge
2 Park Square, Milton Park, Abingdon, Oxon, OX14 4RN

Routledge is an imprint of the Taylor & Francis Group, an informa business

© 2019 Taylor & Francis

Library of Congress Cataloging-in-Publication Data
A catalog record for this title has been requested

ISBN: 978-1-138-35258-2 (hbk)
ISBN: 978-1-138-55231-9 (pbk)
ISBN: 978-1-315-14809-0 (ebk)

Typeset in Palatino
by Apex CoVantage, LLC

Printed in Canada

Contents

Meet the Authors

Todd Whitaker is a professor of educational leadership at the University of Missouri at Columbia and professor emeritus at Indiana State University. Prior to moving into higher education he was a math teacher and basketball coach in Missouri. Todd then served as a principal at the middle school, junior high, and high school levels. He was also a middle school coordinator in charge of staffing, curriculum, and technology for the opening of new middle schools. He has spent his life pursuing his love of education by researching and studying effective teachers and principals.

One of the nation's leading authorities on staff motivation, leading change, as well as teacher and principal effectiveness, Todd has written over 50 books including the national best seller, *What Great Teachers Do Differently*. Other titles include *Your First Year, Shifting the Monkey, Dealing With Difficult Teachers, 10 Minute*

Inservice, The Ball, What Great Principals Do Differently, Motivating & Inspiring Teachers, and *Dealing With Difficult Parents.*

Todd is married to Beth, also a former teacher and principal, who is a professor of educational leadership at the University of Missouri. They are the parents of three children: Katherine, Madeline, and Harrison.

Madeline Whitaker Good is currently a middle school math teacher in Springfield, Missouri. Prior to moving to middle school, Madeline was an elementary school teacher in two different school districts. She was raised in Terre Haute, Indiana, and graduated from the Peabody College of Education at Vanderbilt University with a Bachelor of Science Degree in Elementary Education and Child Studies. She received the Dorothy J. Skeel Award for Outstanding Professional Promise in Elementary Education. She completed her Master of Education Degree in Educational Leadership and Policy Analysis from the University of Missouri at Columbia as well as her elementary and secondary principal certification. She also co-authored the best-selling book *Your First Year: How to Survive and Thrive as a New Teacher* with Todd Whitaker and Katherine Whitaker.

Katherine Whitaker is currently a high school math teacher in Kansas City, Missouri. She was raised in Terre Haute, Indiana, and received her Bachelor of Science Degree in Secondary Mathematics Education from the University of Missouri. Her first three years in the classroom were spent at the middle school level teaching Math, Algebra, and Reading. She has taught Algebra A, Algebra I, and Algebra II Honors at the high school level. Katherine graduated with her Master of Science in Educational Leadership K-12 from Northwest Missouri State University. She also co-authored the best-selling book *Your First Year: How to Survive and Thrive as a New Teacher* with Todd Whitaker and Madeline Whitaker Good.

Introduction

Confidence. An abstract concept that many are constantly striving for. What if someone came up to you and asked you to describe what a confident person looked like? Take a moment to think about how you would respond. Maybe someone who stands with their head held high? Someone who takes pride in themselves? Someone who isn't afraid to say what they think? Even if we chose different scenarios to place this confident person in, there is a good chance that all of our descriptions would have similar themes connecting them. Most people have a general idea or vision about what a confident person looks like, talks like, moves like, etc.

Now, let's say this same someone asked you to explain how you plan on *becoming* confident. What would you say then? Maybe sign up for a public speaking class? Dress nicer? Ignore negative self-talk? Even if we discussed this all day, there is a good chance we would never come to a consensus about how one can *become* confident. It is easy to identify and describe confidence, but difficult to cultivate it. If you Google "How to become confident," you'll find that the explanations many give are vague. Therefore, how are we supposed to become confident when even the directions to do so are abstract?

Classroom management. An abstract concept that many teachers are constantly striving for. What if someone came up to you and asked you to describe what an effectively managed classroom looked like? A class where every student is calm? Where every student is engaged? Where every student feels welcome? Even if we chose different classroom scenarios, just like when we described confidence, there is a good chance that all of our descriptions would have similar themes connecting them. We can all picture effective classroom management in some capacity.

Now, let's say this person asked you to explain how you plan on *becoming* a great classroom manager. What would you say then? Implement procedures? Build relationships with students?

Enforce rules? Great plan! So how do you decide what procedures are actually important? What is your plan for students that you cannot win over? How will you handle a student who breaks a rule?

We bet that most educators, from pre-service to retired, could agree that classroom management is one of the make-or-breaks of teaching. It impacts nearly all aspects of your school day, and may even fill your weekends with stress and worry. So why is answering that question so difficult? **How do you plan on** *becoming* **a great classroom manager?** Shouldn't we have figured this out by now? Shouldn't there be a 5- or 10-step plan to get every teacher to that point? You would think so, but being an educator means you are working with people, and people are complicated. Some believe that if you *just* built relationships or *just* had better lesson plans, everything would fall into place. However, we all know that it is never that simple.

Our first book, *Your First Year* (2016), was written to help beginning teachers survive and thrive during their initial year. Although this book covers a variety of situations first year teachers face, an essential portion of the book is dedicated to effectively managing a classroom. We know this can be a major stumbling block for novice teachers, as it was for us! After listening, talking, and working with teachers, we realized that classroom management is something that affects teachers from their 1st year to their 30th. That is why we felt the need to write this book. With that being said, we realized that this book needed to be different.

Although there are a vast number of classroom management resources readily available for educators, some of which we even reference in this book, we felt there was still something being left out of the discussion. We have decided that we are no longer putting on the facade of the perfect classroom or the perfect teacher. To be completely honest, there are days we do not even take our own advice because teaching is hard and working with people, especially young people, can be complicated and unpredictable. Social media, administrators, central office, other teachers, and the public occasionally perpetuate this misbelief that classrooms can and should be perfect, even if they never outright say 'it needs to be perfect.'

Our goal with this book and the ideals within are about promoting effectiveness, not perfectness. We are not here to share the "silver bullet" of classroom management. Spoiler alert: there isn't one! When it seems too good to be true, it generally is. We are here, however, to show that whether you are in the beginnings of your career or near the end, you can become a better classroom manager. We are going to work to make the abstract concept as concrete as possible, give practical advice on dealing with difficult situations, and show that even after your worst day, there is still hope for tomorrow. Our goal with classroom management is similar to our overall objective in teaching: we are in the improvement business, not the perfection business.

As a final thought before we begin, we understand that there are a variety of philosophies of and reactions to "classroom management." We are not here to discuss the different belief systems behind management techniques, nor are we here to soliloquize about the different types of management structures that teachers use. As mentioned previously, there is no one-size-fits-all solution to everyone's management woes. Instead, we are here to help you understand the concept of classroom management in a concrete way, identify areas for improvement, and gain practical tools. We hope that from the moment you set the book down, whether you are having small classroom setbacks or major management woes, you can apply some of this advice immediately. Just like everything in teaching, change begins with you. So let's start your change toward improvement (versus perfection) right now.

1

House Metaphor

Although this book is about managing a classroom, we aren't going to begin the story in a school. Instead, we want you to picture yourself in a house. Not just any house, however. We want you to picture your dream house. Whether you currently live in a house, apartment, condo, mobile home, or even an RV, we can all picture what our ideal home *would* have. Think about both the practical and frivolous parts that you would want. What is the floor plan? How many stories, bedrooms, and bathrooms? What is the overall architecture? Contemporary, Victorian, Art Deco? What about the fun stuff? Pool, game room, or even an indoor basketball court?

In this book we are going to discuss classroom management in the context of this house you pictured. To build and maintain a house you need three main things: a strong foundation, the actual house structure, and regular upkeep. When thinking about managing a classroom, you also need three things: strong relationships, high and clear expectations, and consistency. Since we all have now visualized our house, the house metaphor introduced below will be our first step in making the abstract concept of classroom management become clearer and more concrete for everyone.

The Foundation—Relationships

When building a house, the foundation comes first. If a house is built correctly, the foundation will be strong on the 70 degree and sunny days, and will continue to maintain on the severe-thunderstorm-warning days. This is just like your classroom. When relationships are built correctly, those bonds will be there to help you celebrate on your best days of teaching, but also keeps your classroom cohesive on your worst. When becoming a great classroom manager, you need to place relationships at the forefront. Relationships with your students are like the strong and solid foundation of a house. According to Emmer and Saborine (2015), "building positive relationships with students should be a primary focus of preventative efforts" when it comes to classroom management (p. 27). As cited by Emmer and Saborine (2015), research has shown that positive student-teacher relationships not only positively affect student attitudes and learning (Cornelius-White, 2007; Roorda, Koomen, Spilt, & Oort, 2011), but also have direct ties to teacher burnout and overall job satisfaction (Chang, 2009; Friedman, 2006; Klassen & Chiu, 2010).

The Structure—High and Clear Expectations

Now, it is actually time to build the house itself. This is the house that you will see every day—the one that you will live in. Thus, just like you wanted to have a strong foundation to build upon, you also want a solid, functional, and livable house. A clear floor plan that works for you with rooms sized and shaped just the way you want. So what would a solid, functional, and livable classroom look like? Would it have kindergarteners crawling all over the ground while you are teaching an important literacy lesson? Would it have 10th graders having a conversation about last night's party when they are supposed to be analyzing poetry? Of course not! This is why having high and clear behavioral expectations is an additional aspect of strong behavior management skills.

According to Bridget Hamre and Robert Pianta (2006), it is critical for schools and teachers to maintain high behavioral expectations to go along with positive teacher-student relationships. Even if you do not end up in a setting where these assumptions are school-wide, you are the person who makes expectations in your classroom. If you do not expect kindergarteners to sit quietly during a lesson—then they won't. If you do not expect your 10th graders to stay focused on a task—then they won't. Make sure that you are the teacher that expects your students to behave their best, and explains explicitly what that looks like. Therefore, you and your students know the difference between what is appropriate and what is not.

The Maintenance—Consistency

Picture this: you now have your house built. It is built on a sturdy foundation, and looks beautiful with its brick exterior and welcoming front porch. You absolutely love living in it, and you cannot imagine moving out. Then one day, you have a leaky faucet in your upstairs bathroom. You think to yourself, "Hmm . . . this is just a leaky faucet. Not a huge issue—I will fix it later." In two weeks, you now have hard water build up around your leaky faucet. Even though you are disappointed, you still think of that issue as minor, and decide you will get back to it another time. After one month, you walk into a back room of your house that you rarely visit, and find a wet mark on the ceiling. You run upstairs and discover that your leaky faucet has more issues than you thought—and now you are left dealing with broken plumbing, a ruined floor, and even a damaged ceiling! In that moment, you realize that you should have just fixed that leaky faucet when you first found it.

This story finalizes our metaphor of the house that we built. The foundation of the house is the relationships, and the actual house we live in each day is the expectations that we have. Now, how do we keep the house running smoothly? Regular basic upkeep, like fixing a leaky faucet. In the classroom, this regular upkeep represents consistency. This consistency applies to both relationships and expectations. So our challenge is working to do the right thing on a day-to-day basis because taking care of your classroom (and taking care of a house) can take a lot of regular upkeep.

* * *

We want you to use this metaphor as a starting point to help build, affirm, or reconstruct your understanding of classroom management. With that being said, we are not here to tell you exactly how your dream house, or your classroom management structures and systems, should look. Every teacher is different and every classroom is different. Thus, only you can decide how this will play out in your classroom. What we want to do is give you the building blocks to be able to start thinking about classroom management in a slightly different way. We want to affirm positive techniques you are already using and simultaneously empower you to change what needs to be adjusted.

Tweaks and Resets

As we discuss the different aspects of the house you will be building, we are also going to discuss what to do when things don't go as planned. There can be a lot of things that cause a house to crumble. An unstable foundation. Shaky at best floor joists. A plumber who was not as qualified as they claimed to be. Sometimes it can be something as unpredictable as a tornado or hurricane. The same can be said for your classroom. Maybe you received a class of students who seemed to be mortal enemies with each other from the day they walked into your classroom. Maybe you had to implement a new technology initiative that threw off the expectations you are normally able to explain so clearly. Maybe you can't seem to figure out how strict you should be in enforcing your cell phone policy. Maybe three new students showed up at your door on the first day of state testing. No matter what happened, there can be times when you are standing in the middle of class and you realize something is not going well. Sometimes it is a small thing, like a lesson structure or a seating arrangement. Other times, it feels like literally everything in your class is a disaster. So what can you do about it?

Tweaks

Let's imagine that you are not pleased with how one specific part of your day has been going. For example, each day you are struggling with the transition from lunch to learning. Your students come in boisterously and it seems like a "battle royale" just to get them to focus. Your initial instinct may be to talk to the entire class about behaving more appropriately. Rather than reactively telling the entire group of students what they are doing wrong, we want you to become reflective about what *you* can do to come up with a long-term solution. For example, you could change your behavior or a structure within your classroom to see if that makes a difference. In the end, the only behavior you can truly control is your own. Let's say you decided that starting tomorrow, you will find a way to more clearly state your expectations after lunch, whether that is teaching them a song that they sing as they transition into the classroom or a visual reminder of expectations on the board. That way, you know there is absolutely no confusion about what students need to do when they step into your classroom.

This strategy is called a *tweak*. A tweak is a small change you make to improve something that is not going well in your classroom. Tweaks are something that effective teachers do regularly all day long. Usually it involves a change in the behavior of the teacher with the objective being a resulting change in the behavior of the students. Typically tweaks are implemented to prevent something from occurring again rather than as a negative response to something that has already happened. Sometimes tweaks are in regard to a lesson, like when you are in the middle of teaching something but you realize it is not coming out clearly, so you try a different approach. Other times tweaks are used in response to student behavior issues, which are the situations we will be addressing in this book. Because it is a tweak, communication is optional. You do not have to inform/announce to the students that anything is changing. Even though your students often realize

> Typically tweaks are implemented to prevent something from occurring again rather than as a negative response to something that has already happened.

you may be implementing different expectations, you approach it in such a positive tone that they will not make the connection that the decision came from a reaction to their behavior. Instead you tweak *your* behavior in order to prevent misbehavior that was occurring previously.

Reset

Now let's imagine that there are more than a few things that are going wrong. Not occasionally, or after an assembly, or on a really nice Friday, but pretty much every day. Each time the students enter your class they are out of control. Seemingly every time you teach a lesson, students are unengaged and disruptive. You have been using tweaks for the past couple of weeks, but the culture and climate of your classroom has become too ingrained for these small changes to truly affect anything. You go home every day at a loss about what to do next. When your classroom begins to look or feel like this, tweaks are usually no longer an option.

When you hit the point where you can no longer be the teacher you wanted to be, it is time for a reset.

When you hit the point where you can no longer be the teacher you wanted to be, it is time for a reset. If the climate and culture of the classroom has hit this point, that usually means that either the foundation is cracked, the structure is not as high and clear as it needs to be, or we have not maintained our classroom like we should have. Sometimes only one of these is the issue, but sometimes it is all three things. The differences between a "tweak" and the "reset button" are significant.

Tweak	Reset
• Unlimited • Small/medium-sized adjustments • Optional communication • Can be planned or made in the moment	• Limited, 1–2 times in a year • Large changes in relationships, expectations, rules, procedures, consistency, and classroom culture • Mandatory communication • Must be planned in advance

You can hit your "reset button" anytime, but it may be most effective after a holiday break, after a 3-day weekend, or on a Monday. In many schools, there may be natural opportunities with a new grading period or semester which may involve different students in the class. It does not matter, as long as you have taken the time to really reflect on what changes are needed. When you reset, you should reset *everything* that is not working since this may be your only chance to do these alterations. When you hit the reset button, you want a "fresh start." If you begin this new phase with, "You guys have been so terrible . . ." is it really giving you and your students this new beginning? Instead, if the adjustments can be centered on your class's future rather than on the past, you have a better chance of a successful reset.

The Silver Lining

We cannot emphasize the importance of tweaks and resets enough. Whether you are in your 1st or 31st year of teaching, it can be demoralizing when your classroom has not turned out how you imagined it. On our worst days filled with student misbehavior, truly the only thing that gives us hope is knowing that tomorrow we can do something that may potentially make the situation better. Tweaks and the reset provide us with that silver lining. This is why you will see a tweak section in each of the following chapters. We want you to understand the three aspects of the house metaphor conceptually, but then we want to show you how to adjust situations in your own classroom right now using tools we have introduced.

As for the reset, we will be addressing this fully in Chapter 6. We are including this near the end of the book because we feel it is the last resort when it comes to classroom management. You cannot reset your classroom until you have a strong understanding of relationships, expectations, and consistency. We also feel that the majority of classroom issues can be solved through the use of tweaks. Giving you the foundational knowledge is first and foremost. Second comes the ability to continually tweak if something is not functioning the way you want it to. Last resort would be the reset. In that chapter there will be scenarios, thought processes, and language to use if a reset needs to be implemented.

Every bad situation has the possibility to get better, but the only way anything will change is if you continue to try. Although we are going to give you in-depth examples of how to make changes to improve your classroom management abilities, there is no "magic potion" that can fix everything. We are not here to try to get you to buy a boxed curriculum that guarantees a fix in student misbehavior. We all know that any salesperson who knocks on your door with that promise probably should not be let inside. Instead, what we are going to share is how we, as practicing educators, work to prevent and handle misbehavior when it inevitably arrives in our rooms. No matter how you feel right now, whether it is motivated, defeated, or even indifferent, all we ask is that you try, try, and try again. There are a lot of variables in our classrooms that we cannot control as teachers and educators; however, the one variable we can control is ourselves.

2

Effective Planning and Instruction

Foundational Understanding of the Concept

Before we jump into the house metaphor in a deeper way, we would be foolish not to discuss how any classroom management system would be set up to fail without effective planning. When we picture classroom management, it can be easy to imagine that most of it pertains to dealing with in-the-moment student misbehavior. Although that is one aspect of it, the most effective teachers are those who try to structure their classroom and lessons in a way that will help *prevent* student misbehavior (Whitaker, 2012; Emmer, Evertson, & Anderson, 1980). Since this book is written through the lens of classroom management, we will focus our discussion about lesson planning and instruction around two main concepts: organization and engagement. When we discuss organization, we will center the conversation around your classroom's physical environment and lesson structures. In regard to engagement, we will give you practical advice that will help your lessons keep students actively interested, so potential misbehaviors will be minimized.

Personal Reflection—Madeline

During my first year of teaching 8th grade math, I had a student who would enter my classroom every day and loudly state, "UGH. I HATE this class." Coming from teaching 3rd grade the few years before, I found this to be a jarring statement for me to hear over and over again when class started. In 3rd grade I definitely had students who preferred certain subjects over others, and those who would groan when we had to stop reading or doing a science lesson, but I had never had a student so adamantly state that he or she hated my class. Every day. Over and over.

I pride myself in being a very purposeful teacher who has high expectations but also builds relationships well. I rarely (if ever) raise my voice, and I try to make learning math as fun as possible. So when this student came in *every day* and said that, it eventually wore me down. I took it personally. My feelings got hurt. I was losing motivation to even continue to try and teach that student if he hated me so much.

One day, I hit my limit. He had said it one too many times. At the end of the day, I went upstairs and found the student waiting outside to get picked up from school. I pulled him aside and finally told him how I had been feeling. I explained that when he says that every day, it hurts my feelings. I explained that he knows how much I care about him and how he knows that I am always willing to change things in class to make it better. If he would tell me what could be improved upon, I would do it (I had already sent out my first quarter survey to get feedback, and he hadn't written anything helpful).

When I finished speaking, he stood there for a few seconds to process his thoughts, and then spoke. "Mrs. Good, it's not that I don't like you or even your class. Math is just *hard*. I actually like you and your class, I just suck at math. It hurts my brain and gives me a headache. I promise I won't say it again." His mom pulled up right after he said that, so we quickly wrapped up our conversation and I walked back into school. In that moment, I realized that this student's daily disruptions were not caused by a poor relationship, low expectations, or a lack of consistency. The house metaphor had nothing to do with it. Instead, it stemmed from his understanding, or lack thereof, of the subject matter. I was managing my class effectively, but my instruction needed to change.

I wanted to share this story to explain why we are including an entire chapter about instruction. Although the three aspects of the house metaphor are *key* to improving your classroom management abilities, we cannot ignore the importance of making sure your lessons are organized and engaging. The student who hated my class felt like he couldn't be successful, which then caused him to act out on a daily basis. Some misbehaviors will occur because of ineffective instruction. Period.

Once I adjusted my instruction with this student, did he instantly become an Albert Einstein and understand all aspects of math that had been confusing him over the past 13 years of his life? Of course not. But after that conversation, and after I worked to improve certain aspects of my instruction, he never came in and told me he hated my class again. With two weeks of school left, he even told me that I was his favorite teacher. No joke. Although not every story ends up with a happy ending like this one did (we all have many that don't), we have to enjoy the ones that do. We have to never lose sight of the fact that things *can* improve over time. Sometimes we just have to admit where we are making mistakes and then take steps to fix them.

How-to and Application

Organization

First, to be an effective manager you must be thoughtful about your organizational methods. Being organized not only helps prevent potential student misbehavior, it also protects instructional and learning time that is otherwise lost in disorganized classrooms (Stronge, 2007). When we talk about organization, we address it under two subcategories: physical organization and lesson organization. When we discuss physical organization, we will be talking about classroom arrangement, furniture, and materials. When we discuss lesson organization, we will focus around having a plan for each day and preventing down time.

Physical Organization

With regard to furniture, it is important to focus on classroom flow, functionality, and structure. Many of the basic classroom management issues can be addressed even before students enter the classroom by making sure the furniture is set up in a functional way (Jones, 2013). Thus, begin by thinking through these major questions: How many students will you have? Do you have enough desks or tables? What configuration will help you be most successful from day one? Your class size may have a large influence in how your room will be set up.

Ms. George is a middle school science teacher with 30–35 students in each class. She was placed in one of the smallest classrooms in the school, and this, paired with her large class sizes, limits her options on how to design the space. She is also a bit nervous about managing a class that large, so she is looking for a classroom set-up that will be beneficial as she introduces her classroom expectations and procedures with students. The best option for Ms. George is to start the year off with her desks in evenly spaced and orderly rows. This will allow movement between desks to be seamless as she walks around to help individual students. In addition, this arrangement will limit student interaction. Even though Ms. George really wants her desks in groups so students can collaborate during labs, she knows that she can introduce a different desk arrangement at any time. Her main goal at the start of the year is seamless implementation of structure and order. Once she establishes her procedures and routines, she then can move the desks into groups because it is always easier to become less structured than to become more structured.

Mr. Grant is an elementary teacher with 25 students, and he has a fairly large classroom. Because of the extra space, he can be more flexible in how he designs his classroom set-up. He feels confident about placing his desks in groups because most of the whole-class instruction will be done on the carpet. Thus, he decides to group the 25 desks into pods of 5, keeping the area in front of the board open for his carpet, and then reserving the back corner by the window for the classroom library. He arranged his room so that during small group instruction he could still monitor the students he is not directly working with. Even though Mr. Grant has more flexibility to be creative, his main focus is still flow, functionality, and structure—it just looks dissimilar to Ms. George's because his classroom, students, needs, and comfort level are different.

When you are setting up your classroom furniture, the final, and maybe the most important, thing to think through is making sure that you will be able to observe all students at all times, no matter where you are instructing from. If Ms. George has one desk hidden behind a file cabinet, or if Mr. Grant's reading nook is nestled behind the technology center, both teachers have set up a situation that could turn sour quickly. There would be places that students could go in the classroom and be "hidden." Now, there is a chance that Mr. Grant and Ms. George could have a class of perfect angels that would never ever take advantage of those "hidden gems," but as teachers, we would not take that risk. It would be much easier to be proactive about those possible issues than to be reactive and have to deal with the behavior later.

The second aspect of physical organization is the materials that you will be working with. Make sure that necessary and regularly used materials are easily accessible, while less-frequented materials are stored away in an organized fashion that allows you to retrieve them when the time comes. What are things that you and your students will need on a day-to-day basis? Pencils? Notebooks? Textbooks? What are things that you and your students may not need as regularly, but should still be accessible? Scissors? Calculators? Math manipulatives? There is also a chance you have materials that you do not need to access regularly, whether you are a new teacher that simply doesn't know what certain items are, or you are a seasoned teacher who saves the old curriculum guides because you love a few of the lessons in them. Either way, make sure these materials are not wasting precious easily accessible storage space that could be used in a more effective way.

When Mrs. Smith, a 3rd grade teacher, was preparing her classroom, she made sure each student had a dry erase board and a clipboard in their seat pocket because in her mind those were going to be used regularly. She placed their binders, however, in their locker cubbies, because those would probably be used less frequently. When it came to notebooks, she was entirely unsure if she would use them at all at the beginning of the year, so she put them neatly in a cabinet that she could easily reach when the time was right.

Although Mr. Jenkins is a high school English teacher, he too thought through placement of materials. He knew that most students would come in on day one with a spiral notebook, but he has many extras near his desk just in case. He also has put spare sharpened pencils in a cup on his desk so students could get one if they forgot, but also placed a sign-out sheet to keep track of them so at the end of the period he could collect those that he lent out. Finally, on the cabinets below his window, he has organized charging stations for students' personal devices so they would be in a safe yet easily accessible location.

Lesson Organization

The second aspect of being an organized teacher is in regard to lessons. Obviously all of you reading this teach a variety of grade levels, skill levels, and subject areas, therefore diving into a discussion about best practices specific to a certain age or topic would not serve the book's larger purpose. Instead, remember that we are discussing each of these topics through the lens of classroom management, and we have found that there are two major techniques that ineffective teachers do not implement in their classrooms.

Prioritizing the First Five Minutes

For many teachers who struggle with classroom management, their difficulties begin the moment that students walk into the classroom. Sometimes the issues are subtle, like students not getting started quickly. Other times, they are more obvious, with students loudly protesting doing work that day and even trying to convince the teacher to change that day's plans. The best teachers set the tone from the moment students walk into the classroom by having a set routine that gets students in the mindset of work that day. We call this the "first five minutes." This prevents students from coming into class with the idea that they will not be getting work done, and it sets a clear mes-

> **The best teachers set the tone from the moment students walk into the classroom by having a set routine that gets students in the mindset of work that day.**

sage that even if students come in wanting to avoid work, their best efforts at work avoidance are for naught.

Your "first five minutes" should focus around efficiency and productivity, and should always be academic in nature (Lemov, 2010). These three characteristics will set the tone for your classroom and your students. For example, in an elementary classroom the "first five minutes" could be the first five minutes of the reading block. In one classroom, students may know that at the beginning of every reading block, they should go to their carpet spots to read and discuss a book as a class. In the class next door maybe their "first five minutes" is saved for independent reading. In the classroom down the hall, their "first five minutes" may instead be structured time where the teacher reminds students of that day's station structure and answers any pressing questions. All three of these examples would prepare those students for what is to come during that day's reading block as long as the teacher consistently kept that routine.

In a secondary classroom, the "first five minutes" generally means the first five minutes of that class. Just like in an elementary classroom, the routine must be efficient, productive, and academically focused, but it could look entirely different. For example, maybe a math teacher consistently begins their lesson with a bell-ringer question that reviews something that was learned previously during the year. On the other hand, an American History teacher may always begin class by discussing that week's current events. A special education teacher may find that using these first minutes for goal setting with their students is the best use of time because it helps get students focused on and prepared for what is to come.

Even if you have the best "first five minutes" plan, you are still going to have occasional days where students ask, "Do we have to do work today?". Or a day where they will try to get you off task by asking random questions about some YouTube video you just HAVE to show the class. No matter what tricks they try to throw your way, do not let them distract you from those ever-important "first five minutes." Stick to your routine. Think of it as setting a professional or business-like tone in your classroom. When a teacher goes into—or starts off with—a business tone, the students generally follow suit. However, if the teacher does not do this consistently or in an appropriate way, there is almost no chance that the students will enter and begin class with that efficient, ready to go, mindset.

Now, we would be lying if we said that we began literally every single class period, from the first day of school to the last, with some type of productive and academic structure. With that said, the days where this does not occur are very few and far between. They only happen because of bizarre school day schedules, standardized testing, or end-of-the-year assemblies and activities. Making your first five minutes of class predictable and consistent for the large majority of your school year paves the way for learning to occur and management issues to stay at a minimum.

Avoiding "Down Time"

The second aspect of having organized lessons is simple: avoid "down time." By that, we mean that your students should have something meaningful and purposeful to do every moment of every block, period, or lesson. Although we think students should be able to inherently know that they should find something quiet to complete if they find themselves without anything to do, we all know that that is not reality. We feel confident that even as adults, if we were given unstructured time during a class or professional development session, there is a good chance we wouldn't use it wisely! Remember the likelihood of a group of students using the last 15 minutes of class to 'talk quietly amongst yourselves' can easily be an

> By that, we mean that your students should have something meaningful and purposeful to do every moment of every block, period, or lesson.

invitation for disaster. At that point, unfortunately, we have to go into a reactive mode rather than a more desirable preventative one. Keep in mind that planned breaks that are purposeful and structured do not fall into the category of "down time." When working with children and young adults, short and intentional breaks can make the remainder of your lesson more productive and meaningful.

Down time is dangerous for two reasons. First, it is a waste of precious instructional time. Many educators agree that there are not enough hours in the day to teach students everything they need. Thus, every single minute should be planned for because even five wasted minutes each day of school leads to hours of lost instructional time over a school year. If you are teaching a first grader how to read, or an 8th grader how to do a proper push-up, minutes gained by being highly organized could lead to increased understanding of the material (Taylor et al., 1999). The second reason that down time is dangerous is that it causes a break in structure. As educators, we know that the most effectively run classrooms are ones with tight structures that help students succeed. If you are teaching a lesson, but somehow you planned it to where only three-quarters of the class is participating, what are the other students doing? As we mentioned before, some will simply lose focus, which may not be a huge detriment to you, but it could cause those students to miss out on precious learning opportunities. Others, however, may use that "down time" to distract classmates, check their social media feeds, or even disrupt the teacher. Once one student has lost focus in one way or another, the likelihood of others joining in is high.

To prevent such issues, you must be sure to plan and prepare your lessons beforehand. Consider what your students will be doing from the moment they walk into your room to the moment they leave it. We know that it may seem obvious to some of you, but the reality is that there are teachers who do not make this a priority. Avoiding down time by having effectively prepared lessons can also positively influence student achievement (Stronge, 2007). So how do you do this? If your "first five minutes" are already in place, you then need to think about the actual structure of the lesson that day. Put yourself in the place of three types of students: the student who you know will take a long time to complete work, the student who gets things done at an average pace, and the student who is a fast finisher. Are there any moments during your class time that one of the students may not have something meaningful that they must work on? We are not asking you to give the student busy work just to keep him or her quiet. Instead, we want you to think about limiting or eliminating the amount of unplanned and unstructured opportunities in your classroom. Being prepared with appropriate and meaningful activities for any students that work at a differing pace can provide a seamless transition which can avoid 'lag' time for students.

Being prepared with appropriate and meaningful activities for any students that work at a differing pace can provide a seamless transition which can avoid 'lag' time for students.

Maybe you are an AP Physics teacher who uses whole-class direct instruction and discussion as a primary instructional technique. You know that during this part of class you expect students to take notes before moving on to that day's assignment or lab. What do you have planned for students once they finish the assignment or lab? Is there any additional work that needs to be done for that lesson? Possibly an extension task that would push their thinking further, or could they work on something that needs to be done for a different class? Maybe you are a middle school orchestra teacher who needs students to practice their parts in small groups with their sections. Do you have clear guidelines for what this looks like? Is there a chance that your students will take this as looser structure and create "down time" with it? Is there a way that you could give students clear targets or goals that they must achieve before they can move on? No matter what kind of teacher you are, making sure students have purposeful work to complete all class period will be a key preventative technique when it comes to classroom management.

Engaging Instruction

Now that we have covered organization, which is the first half of effective instruction, we need to discuss the second part. We feel that the final piece that makes instruction effective is engagement.

At this point, we want to be very specific about what engagement is and what engagement is not. You might think the only way to keep students engaged while teaching *Paul Revere's Ride* by Henry Wadsworth Longfellow is to bring in a real-life horse, stand on its back, wear full Colonial garb, and recite the entire poem from memory. Although this could work, we know that the feasibility of doing this for every lesson, every day, is next to nil. Instead, we want to introduce the concept of engagement in a more reasonable and practical way.

Engagement means that you work to teach your content in a way that students can actively participate in the lesson every day. As technology has advanced and instructional practices have developed, the idea of "engaging" lessons has at times been interpreted to mean either having students utilize the latest app/tech tool or having students collaborate with each other. Although we do utilize these strategies on our own classrooms to enhance some lessons, they are not the driving force behind what we define engagement to be. We want to simplify the idea of "engaging" for you so it can be understood within the context of classroom management.

> *Engagement* **means that you work to teach your content in a way that students can actively participate in the lesson every day.**

To keep your lessons engaging so student misbehavior is prevented, we recommend focusing on three criteria.

1. **Make sure students have a way to actively participate in each part of the lesson.** As mentioned before, although this could be technology- or collaboration-based, it does not have to be. Engagement can be mental as well as physical. You could have students actively engaged in the lesson by having them work on a shared device with a partner, or you could keep it simple by having students take notes or fill out a graphic organizer that helps them categorize the material in a helpful way. You also can utilize basic but effective instructional techniques such as the "Cold Call," where you call on students throughout the lesson without

having them raise their hands (Lemov, 2010). An additional tried-and-true technique is effective wait time after you ask a question. This ensures that more students will have a chance to process and share their thoughts (Lemov, 2010).

2. **Make sure you have knowledge of, and can capitalize on, student attention spans.** In spite of the fact that there is little research that gives us a conclusive amount of time that students can typically pay attention for, any practicing educator knows that it is generally not the length of the entire class period or subject block (Bunce, Flens, & Neiles, 2010). Consequently, we as teachers need to "chunk" our periods/blocks to make sure that we are not expecting students to stay focused on one task for 90, 70, or even 50 minutes straight. The best teachers use their knowledge of student attention spans when preparing and implementing lessons (Bain & Jacobs, 1990). Think about how you could split your class time into smaller sections, so students are not required to work on one task the entire period. For example, after you finish direct instruction, have students "transition" for 1–2 minutes. This time could be spent having students move from the carpet to their assigned seats, letting students out of their seats to grab necessary materials or assignments, or even giving them a short brain break. As long as you have a clear signal that lets students know when it is time to start working again (like music, chimes, or visible timer), this mental break can help students get ready for the next chunk of class. This is not to say that we should not work to build our students' attention spans, but we do want to acknowledge the reality that even adults get restless when they must sit for extended periods of time at trainings and professional developments.

3. **Make sure your lessons/assignments are clearly understood.** Clarity, or effective oral communication skills, is a quality that effective teachers have (Polk, 2006). If teachers are not clear about content that must be taught or directions that must be followed, there is a good chance that students will begin to misbehave. There are some students

that will simply misbehave for a variety of reasons, no matter the clarity of the teacher. That being said, having clear instructions and directions will help prevent misbehaviors from the large majority of students. In fact, step-by-step instruction for a lesson has been shown to increase student engagement in the material (Emmer et al., 1980). Always remember that one goal is to minimize the number of students that are not on task. We believe that most students come to school wanting to learn. Once guidelines become unclear, misbehavior can potentially begin from boredom or frustration. One way teachers can make their instruction clearer is to explain all steps that students need to take to fully understand the material. Explaining things in more than one way, answering student questions one-on-one or in front of the class, and providing visual supports to pair with the lesson are ways you can be clearer for your students. (For specific tips on how to improve this aspect of your instruction, we recommend reading the article "Principles of Instruction" by Barak Rosenshine [2012].) When thinking about directions, some ways teachers can improve their effectiveness is to have them written or posted on the Smartboard, whiteboard, chalkboard, etc., or on a document students can access. You can also have students reiterate the directions you just gave or show examples of what you are looking for, whether they come from students modeling them or from an example you prepared ahead of time. We will give further tips and examples on how to do this later.

Tweak

Great teachers are constantly adjusting what and how they teach. Not only do they tweak their instruction from year to year, they also do it from week to week, day to day, and even moment to moment. One thing that helps teachers do this continuous adjusting is called "withitness," which is described as being "aware of what is happening in all parts of the classroom at all times" (Brophy, 1996, p. 11). Teachers who are "with-it" can keep a constant pulse of what is going on in the classroom, which allows them to handle student misbehavior. Although this skill is extremely helpful in regard to putting out "small fires," we also want to argue that it gives teachers the larger vision as to when lessons need to be tweaked to improve student behavior. We are going to give you a few examples of how teachers who utilize "withitness" can tweak parts of their lessons to improve student behavior.

Tweaking Organization

Sometimes when a lesson is not going as planned, it is simply because aspects of it were not organized as well as they could have been. Maybe you are a kindergarten teacher who realized (a bit too late) that the location of the crayons and the location of the paper materials did not allow for a smooth flow of student movement during stations. Or you may be a 9th grade math teacher who realized after teaching her first block class that the examples you used were explained in an illogical order. In both of these situations, effective teachers would do some type of tweaking to make sure that the issues were prevented in the future. For example, the kindergarten teacher could restart stations for that day. He could bring students back to their seats or carpet spots, quickly adjust the location of the materials, re-explain and model how students should access them during stations, and then try them again. On the other hand, although the 9th grade teacher has run out of time in her first class, she could reorder the examples for the rest of the classes that she teaches that day and make sure all classes benefit from this new approach tomorrow. Both of these are effective examples of how teachers can tweak aspects of lesson organization that can help prevent student misbehavior.

Tweaking Clarity

Another issue that can cause and perpetuate student misbehavior is lack of clarity. Sometimes students become disruptive because the directions were explained in a muddled way, or because the actual content was not clearly articulated. Not only is teacher clarity important in regard to classroom management, but it also has been found to positively impact student learning and engagement with the instructor and content (Titsworth, Mazer, Goodboy, Bolkan, & Myers, 2015). Many times, special education and English as a second language teachers have some of the best strategies to improve a teacher's clarity because they work with students who have such diverse needs.

For example, maybe you are a 6th grade PE teacher who is trying to get students to warm-up before you begin today's lesson about heart rate. You tell them to "warm-up," but somehow they have forgotten the five different movements you taught them the week before. So instead of doing the warm-up routine you hoped for, it has quickly turned into a mass of students standing there chatting with friends while others are trying to make horseplay a warm-up activity. To fix this, you might need to begin your next few classes (or more than a few depending on how long the lack of clarity has occurred) by modeling their five warm-up choices before sending them off to get started. Eventually you could have students model the warm-up choices for the class. This would help push students to become more independent and give you a better idea of who understands the warm-up and who needs continual reminders.

On the other hand, you may have a lesson that does not go well not because of unclear directions, but because of unclear content instruction. For example, maybe you are a 2nd grade teacher who is trying to teach your students about measuring objects in feet. You teach and model how to measure items in feet, and have students begin practicing with items around the room. As you circulate and help students, you realize that there are some students who are mixing up the concept of feet as a measurement and *actual* feet. Some students have already taken their shoes off and are getting ready to measure their classroom tables by walking across them. In that moment, you realize that you need to tweak your instruction on an individual student basis to clarify any misunderstanding about the word, or you may realize that it is a more widespread misconception that should be addressed in a whole-class discussion or lesson. Remember that when you tweak, you are changing either your own behavior or your classroom expectations to improve the situation. Even though your first instinct may be to lecture the students about everything they are doing wrong, we would recommend approaching it in a more self-focused way. For example, you could start redirecting students by saying, "I am not sure I explained this correctly," rather than lecturing them about their misbehavior.

Tweaking Engagement

The final major way that teachers can tweak lessons using "withitness" is to make adjustments that will increase student engagement. As all practicing teachers know, even some of your best lessons will leave students yawning or asking to do something else. Engaging students consistently is not easy, especially when you are teaching an overly difficult unit or topic. So what can you tweak to increase student engagement in a lesson that is just not going as hoped? Below are a few strategies that can be adapted depending on your grade level, content, and specific student abilities:

◆ **Incorporate movement:** Instead of having students answer questions while writing at their seats, you could post the questions around the walls of the classroom and have students rotate between them.

◆ **Get students talking:** If you notice student interest is starting to wane, go ahead and find a way that could get students chatting, even if it is only for 30 seconds. Have them explain one of their answers to the person sitting next to them, or have them share any questions they currently have about the material.

◆ **Give students a break:** If time allows, you could also simply give students a short break between parts of your class. For younger students, this may be a 'brain break' where they participate in a whole-class game or activity. For older students, it could be a 2-minute transition time where students are allowed to take their phones out or talk to their friends until the timer goes off.

◆ **Utilize "mild pressure":** According to Marzano (2007), putting "mild pressure" on students throughout class can positively impact student engagement and learning (p. 102). This pressure cannot be extreme or implemented for extended periods of time, but if done correctly through strategies like calling on students whether their hands are up or not, or letting students know that they will have a graded 1–2 question quiz at the end of class can cause students to become more invested in the subject matter.

◆ **Implement "mild controversy and competition":** Similar to the previous example, Marzano (2007) recommends that incorporating a moderate level of controversy and/or competition in class can cause students to more deeply engage in the subject matter (p. 103). For example, a 5th grade teacher could facilitate a constructive debate on different strategies that could be used to solve a problem, or a music teacher could design a friendly competition that motivates students to learn their minor scales. No matter how these are incorporated, it is important to note that these must be mild, because if the controversy or competition gets too intense, the strategy backfires for many involved.

What You Can Do Tomorrow

At the end of each chapter, we will list a few changes that you could make tomorrow. We never expect you to change everything overnight; that is not fair or realistic for you or your students! Instead, we want you to think about one part of your classroom that does not sit right with you. Maybe the first five minutes of class always feels like a circus (and not the fun kind). Maybe you struggle transitioning from reading groups to your writing lesson. Maybe you still can't get all of your students to put away their art supplies when the class is over. Pick one part of your day that you want to change, and see if there is a small thing you could implement starting tomorrow to begin that change. Remember, we aren't wanting you to become perfect, we just want you to improve your effectiveness.

1. **Improve Directions.** Explain directions more clearly by having them posted on the board and having students repeat them after your explanation.

2. **Set the Tone.** Use the first five minutes of class wisely and set the business-like tone from the beginning. Let students know that today and every day they are going to learn and learn a lot!

3. **Increase Engagement.** Think of one part of a lesson that tends to lose student engagement and find a way to get them actively involved. Have them take notes, discuss as a class or with a partner, or answer questions with whiteboards or technology to help them actively participate.

4. **Chunk Your Lessons.** Separate your lessons or class periods into smaller chunks to capitalize on student attention spans. If you know that the direct instruction will take 20 minutes, separate it into smaller sections and include mini "breaks" where students can respond/react verbally or nonverbally (hand signals, writing, whiteboards, technology, etc.) to the class, a classmate, or themselves.

5. **Improve Clarity.** Improve your lesson's clarity by incorporating modeling into the lesson. Whether you are explaining a new style of music or introducing the letter "C," be sure that you are providing both verbal and visual explanations that can improve student understanding. Also, be willing to answer questions and clarify misunderstandings you find students bringing up to improve your clarity even more.

3

The Foundation—Building Relationships

Foundational Understanding of the Concept

Although understanding effective instruction is key, we now want to go back to what the heart of the book is about: the house metaphor. Remember that your house is split into three parts: the foundation, the structure, and the maintenance. Those three aspects represent three crucial pieces of effective classroom management: building relationships, having high and clear expectations, and consistency. It's now time to start building your house!

Before you start purchasing the drywall and flooring, a strong foundation must be built. This foundation will carry your house through sunny days with ease, and more importantly hold a stable base during stormy and unpredictable weather. When thinking about classroom management, the foundation of your house represents the relationships you build with students. Strong relationships make easy days breezy, while they also carry you through the days where nothing seems to go right. Although you can technically build a house without a solid foundation, any construction worker would advise you otherwise. The same can be said about relationships with students. Although you can have a classroom management structure in place without having strong relationships, that structure may not stand the test of time.

As mentioned previously in the introduction, there is much research that emphasizes the importance of building relationships. From helping prevent misbehavior to improving student learning and averting teacher burnout, there are so many reasons why building relationships must be a priority in all classrooms (Emmer & Saborine, 2015; Cornelius-White, 2007; Roorda, Koomen, Spilt, & Oort, 2011; Chang, 2009; Friedman, 2006; Klassen & Chiu, 2010). Although it is apparent that building relationships is key to having successful classroom management, we do want to be clear about something: improving your relationships with students is not going to fix ineffective lessons, unclear expectations, or a lack of consistency. Having strong relationships may help you survive a day of chaos, but if every day is chaos, then it will be a battle just to keep strong relationships, let alone get students to learn something. So instead of thinking about relationships as the way to solve your management woes, we want you to focus on the fact that it provides that foundation of purpose. It gives you the "why" of why you show up every day. It brings the emotion into your work, whether you are laughing at a student's joke or crying over their pain. Even though relationships won't help you systematize your learning environment, it will bring the heart into everything you do.

Personal Reflection—Katherine

During my fourth year of teaching, I had a student in one of my math classes who rarely showed up to school. We'll call him "Devon." He was transient. Devon had started the year with me, moved in October to an unaccredited high school in the city, then reappeared sometime in February. He wore the same clothes all week and it was very apparent he was not showering. Students were never mean to him, but they would not sit by him. His fingernails were almost always black from dirt. Devon missed school a lot so I was constantly having to play catch up with him whenever he did show up. He was one of those kids who had potential but his circumstances were really hurting his future self. Working with him was always a challenge because I love to use proximity and really help the kids by getting on their level; however, some days he did not want me (or anyone else) near him.

At this point in my story I am going to pause and assume that you might be imagining one of your students who fits a similar description. I am also going to assume two more things. The first is that the student you are imagining is probably not your favorite student. The second is that the patience you have for said student is running low. I was in a similar place with Devon for a multitude of reasons, yet I was bound and determined to get him to pass my math class. Devon, however, was not making my job easy because he was also seemingly bound and determined not to pass my math class, or any class for that matter. Every day he refused to do the classwork or even take notes during the lessons. This particular story, however, takes place on a day where we were taking a test.

I remember passing the test out to my class and everyone getting started without hesitation. Devon worked for a solid two minutes then put his head down. I slowly made my way over to him, stood near him, and said, "Devon, sit up and continue working on your test please." No response. "Devon, I know you hear me. Sit up." No response. This was my final straw after weeks of fighting with him to take notes. After weeks of getting him to do at least three problems so I could give him partial credit. I was fed up. Quietly, yet sternly I said, "Devon, if you do not sit up right now I am going to have to send you to the office." I remember those words coming out of my mouth and immediately being sick to my stomach. It felt like an empty and pathetic type of threat. This was my fourth year of teaching; however, it was my first year teaching high school and I had yet to send a kid to the office at this school. Was I really going to start with *this* situation? A student refusing to take a test?

I remember Devon mumbled, between his arm and the desk, "Go ahead and send me. I don't care." And he really didn't care, I was positive of that. This test was probably at the very bottom of his life priority list, right along with washing the dirt out from under his fingernails. Again, that sickness of never having sent a student to the office at this school before hit me. On top of that, I felt like his refusal to do my test did not necessarily warrant me calling an escort to take him to the office. I was stuck. I was nervous. I knew my other students were working on their test, but also secretly watching and listening to me. Waiting to see how this situation was going to unfold. I sat down in the desk next to him to collect my thoughts.

I have no idea why I decided this was the next best choice of action, but, boy, am I glad I made this impulsive decision. I took a deep breath to calm myself down because, honestly, I was nervous and beyond frustrated with this kid. Quietly and as sincerely as I possibly could, I whispered, "Devon, is everything okay?" No response. I took another breath and paused for a second. Finally this came out, "Devon, I'm not even mad at you anymore. I'm just worried. I don't even care about this test anymore either. Please sit up so we can talk about what is going on with **you**." Nothing. I was in full panic mode. I redirected, I threatened, I was nice, now what!? Suddenly, he sat up. "Are you okay?" I asked again. He looked over at me. "No," he finally responded. That simple "no" opened a part of his soul to me. He went on to tell me deeply personal issues that were going on in his life. Issues that I could not even imagine. I am not going to disclose Devon's personal experiences in this book, but this is what caused my "Ah-Ha" moment. No wonder he did not care about the math test. No wonder he rarely came to school. No wonder cleanliness was not a top priority for him. This one moment changed the way I talk with my students and I will forever be grateful to Devon for pushing me in my teaching practice.

On that day, Devon revealed to me the most important education "secret" of my career. What he had finally made me realize is that every single child in my room truly wants to learn. I don't care how they act day in and day out, every single child wants to succeed. Every child wants to be good at life and at school. This is when I learned that it's not about being the cool teacher, or the fun teacher, or the easy teacher. It is about being the teacher who *cares*. I have now shared the secret with you. Be the teacher who cares about their students learning. So much so that they also care about the things that may hinder the learning process. Whether it is a learning disability, the inability to read, drug abuse, or issues at home: be the teacher that cares. Cares enough to ask "Are you okay?" instead of "Why haven't you started on your assignment?" That is what Devon taught me that day and this is how you build relationships, especially with the students who seem unreachable. I believe all teachers know they are supposed to care. I also believe all teachers do care. However, not all teachers know how to care effectively enough to build strong relationships with their students, and that is where we need to go next.

How-to and Application

In our collective experiences, we have found that most teachers feel confident that they know how to build relationships. Building relationships and shaping lives was what inspired them to go into teaching in the first place! We have also found, however, that some teachers may not realize how they come across to students. They think they have built relationships with their students, but they may not realize they also do small (or large) things that tear the relationship down.

There is no checklist that one can follow to guarantee that teachers will grow close to their students. This is because building relationships is not a one-time occurrence. It comes from

This is because building relationships is not a one-time occurrence. It comes from every single interaction teachers have with their students every single day.

every single interaction teachers have with their students every single day. Whether it is a, "Hey! How are you?" as the student walks down the hallway, or pausing to take a breath to make sure you don't say something snarky when a student acts out, each of those interactions can bolster or weaken a relationship.

So how do you actually build and maintain relationships? In Part I of the "How-to and Application" section, we have combined research from *Relating to Students: It's What You Do That Counts* by Robert M. Marzane (2011) with practical experience of teachers to give you straight-forward "how-to" advice about what can help you build and maintain relationships with your students. Part II of the "How-to and Application" section is going to cover what you do when the relationship begins to break, whether it be from student behavior, or your own. Building, maintaining, and repairing is all part of the relationship process.

Before we begin, we want to point out that we understand that the realities of the classroom do not allow for the 10-minute (or even sometimes 2-minute) one-on-one conversations that bring people close quickly like what was described in Katherine's previous example. Sometimes our classes have 35 students in them. Sometimes we have so many standards to cover that the idea of building relationships seems almost impossible. Sometimes a student lashes out at us so the *last* thing we care about is building a relationship with him or her. However, we want to give you tips and reminders that there are many things you *can* do to help build and maintain relationships in a variety of situations, without having unrealistic expectations for what a teacher's day is like. The key is that even after a bad day, tough class, or hurtful interaction, we cannot set the idea of "building relationships" aside perpetually. Although it can be tough, we have to remember that without relationships, the foundation to our classroom (and possibly our reason for even becoming educators in the first place) cracks.

Part I: Building Relationships

Although this one seems like a "no brainer," we cannot emphasize enough what Katherine touched upon previously: that you must care about students to build strong relationships. Effective teachers are those who care, and they use that care to build bonds with their students (Peart & Campbell, 1999). We are not asking you to love every student every single day. We are human and our students are human, so there are going to be days when your patience is tested and when you may get irritated with seemingly trivial things. It is totally normal and okay to feel that way. What matters the most, however, is that we still *do* the right things, even if we don't want to. In fact, there is research to support this. "Perhaps the most powerful message from the research is that relationships are a matter of student perception. They have little to do with how a teacher actually feels about students; it's what teachers do that dictates how students perceive those relationships" (Marzano, 2011, p. 82). This is such a great reminder that teachers do not have to live up to the happy-robot-superhero bar that has been set for them to constantly reach. We hope that most teachers enjoy spending time with their students, but we also know that some days you really do need to "fake it 'til you make it." So on both your great and not-so-great days, how do you show that you care every day?

> **What matters the most, however, is that we still do the right things, even if we don't want to.**

Help Students Be Successful

We believe that the vast majority of students want to do well in school. As teachers, we can make it easier or more difficult for them to do well from the moment they walk into the classroom. Effective classroom managers are constantly working to make the material accessible to students so they can be successful at learning when they come to class. Although this may seem like it pertains to instruction more than relationship building, students can sense if a teacher thinks they are "dumb" or "slow" because they are not understanding the material in the way it is taught. Providing proper scaffolding, as described in the "Effective Planning and Instruction" section, helps build trust between the student and teacher because it makes the student feel success in your classroom. Thus, while you spend extra time thinking about how to scaffold instruction to prevent management issues, know that there is a two-fold benefit to your work.

Never Give up on Students

"I'm done with you!" That is a phrase that every teacher has either said or thought about using with one student before. When they refuse to do work day after day, or when they continuously try to push your buttons just to see if you will react. Eventually, we all hit a breaking point. Even though these situations are so incredibly frustrating, we cannot ever be entirely "done" with a student. You can be "done" with a student for a day, or even a few days, but part of teaching is giving students second chances (and third and fourth and fifth chances). Many times, the students who are pushing your buttons the most are doing it just to see if you will give up on them. No matter if a student refuses to do work on Monday, we have to try again on Tuesday. Can we ever guarantee that the student will come back to school willing to do work? Of course not, but we do have an obligation to always try.

Be Compassionate

It can be hard to remember that students are human beings just like us, especially when they are particularly negative, hateful, or belligerent one day. We recommend that you work to always approach students with compassion, whether they are your nicest or most difficult students. Research has shown that students prefer teachers who show understanding during their interactions with students (Stronge, 2007). For example, when a student isn't doing work, we as teachers tend to try to solve the problem by asking a question like, "Why aren't you doing anything?" To show more compassion, you could instead ask, "Is everything okay?" like Katherine described in her personal example. Either way, you will be able to figure out why the student wasn't doing her work, but the second way leads with compassion instead of accusation, which gets you the information you need without the combative tone. Another example of this is validating students when you are in the middle of a tense behavior management situation. If a student is upset about something, the first thing you could say is, "I believe that is frustrating" or "I understand why you are angry." Although you may still need to provide a consequence for the misbehavior, by leading with compassion you are making the student feel heard and understood. This can go a long way to help diffuse a situation while also maintaining the relationship in a tense moment.

Show Interest in Students' Lives

We recommend choosing 1–2 students each day, and having a brief (keyword!) personal interaction with those students sometime during the school day. Pause and think about the moments throughout your day that are low-stress enough where you can give your full attention to a student for 15–60 seconds. During passing period? If you have lunch or recess duty? Once the class is settled into independent tasks? After you drop students off at a related arts class? Once you are able to identify those low-stress moments, prioritize the student(s) you would like to interact with, and think of topics you could bring up. Sometimes you can just say a comment like, "I like your shoes," or, "You sounded great in the concert last week!" Other times, you could ask a question like, "How did your competition go last night?" or, "What music do you normally listen to?" These brief but personal interactions can go a long way in bringing you closer to your students.

Listen to Your Students

Teachers forget, including ourselves, how unbelievably perceptive our students can be. Just like we can tell if someone is truly listening to us, students can tell as well. In fact, one of the main aspects of an effective teacher is their ability to actively listen to students (Stronge, 2007). You probably listen to students all day every day, but we want to share a scenario with you that may challenge your view of whether or not you are truly listening.

Let's pretend you are inputting your attendance at your desk when a student comes up and wants to tell you something about his or her weekend. In the typical classroom, we would see three general responses:

Response 1: You pause what you are doing to fully listen, then resume working on the attendance once the student is done sharing.

Response 2: You ask the child to hold on so you can finish filling in the attendance, then once you finish they have your undivided attention.

Response 3: You continue working on the attendance as the student tells you about their weekend.

If you feel like you could make each option work in your classroom, then we ask you to put yourself in their shoes for a moment. Let's pretend you walk into your principal's office to tell them a story or ask for help. Read through the responses again, but in the mindset of teacher and principal who is answering an email. Which response would most likely make you feel heard by your principal? Which option would most likely make you feel devalued? We hope that you have come to the conclusion that either response 1 or 2 would make you feel closer to your school leader, whereas response 3 would potentially cause a set-back in the relationship.

Sometimes students are going to come up to you and want to share something and it will not be the right time to do so. We understand that. We also understand that sometimes you simply *do* finish filling out the attendance while the student is telling the story because you know that the kindergartener may not remember whether you listened or not on that Friday morning. We are not asking you to pause everything you are doing every moment a student wants or needs to tell you something. All we are asking for is that you always work to be conscious of the attention you are giving your students. Over time, if students continually feel unheard, it can build a rift in your relationships with them.

Positive Contact to the Home

Every student comes to school wanting to find some sort of success, and the more adults in their lives that can celebrate these successes, the more meaningful it can feel. It is one thing for teachers to tell students how proud they are of them, but it's an entirely different thing to tell those students' parents or guardians. Contacting the adults that your students live with, whether it's dad, step-mom, auntie, grandpa, cousin, etc., gives the student a chance to carry their feeling of success out of your classroom and even out of school.

Different ways you can contact a student's home is via phone call, personal letter, email, professional digital messaging system, positive postcard, or even a positive office referral. Just remember that the more personal you make the contact, the more impactful it could be on the student and the family. If it can improve a student's life and a family's dynamic, even if just for one night, it is worth it. There is a good chance the student will come to school the next day with a more positive outlook on you and your class (Whitaker & Fiore, 2016).

Consistently Be Friendly

Although this one sounds so simple, it probably is the most important piece of advice that teachers should take. For some, it may even seem like the most difficult of the tips because of the commitment required to see it through. Act friendly doesn't mean "act friendly when you remembered your coffee that morning," or "act friendly when the students come to class ready to learn," or "act friendly on certain days of the week—i.e. the Friday before Spring Break." It means act friendly every day.

There have been times when we have caught ourselves not acting friendly as consistently as we could, so we have to make clear reminders for ourselves to try and live this goal consistently. Some examples that we have used are smile more, say hi to students when they come into the classroom, and react with laughter more than frustration. These small acts, when implemented regularly, create an aura around you and create a classroom culture that students can thrive in. Does it guarantee every student will instantly be close with you? Of course not! But it leaves the door open so students can move closer when they are ready. Remember that building relationships is a marathon, not a sprint.

Part II: Repairing Relationships

No matter how hard you work to consistently build and maintain relationships with your students, eventually something is going to happen that will cause a rift in the bond. Maybe a student has a bad day and takes it out on you or a classmate. They overreact about something or throw a fit. On the flip side, sometimes we as teachers are going to have bad days. Maybe one night we did not get enough sleep, so we react harshly to a situation we normally wouldn't. We snap at a class because they have been disruptive one too many times. We are still upset at what happened with our last class and we consequently overreact to our next group of students. These situations happen to both new and experienced teachers alike, so no matter your years of experience, you need practical tools that can help you recover from these tough situations.

The Student Broke the Relationship. Now What?

We want to begin by discussing situations where the student broke the relationship. Sometimes the rift is caused by a snarky comment, a classroom outburst, or even the teacher feeling taken advantage of. No matter what occurred, we want to give you three tips in how to help students fix the relationship that has been broken.

Forgive and Forget

Sometimes students will do things that hurt your feelings. Sometimes students will do things that make you feel frustrated. Sometimes students will do things that make you straight up mad. No matter what happens, one option you always have is to forgive and forget. Let's say that it's Friday afternoon at dismissal time and a student who seems a little on edge appears close to breaking your expectation that they stay in their seats until they are dismissed. You remind him of what he is supposed to be doing, and he mumbles something inaudible under his breath that makes a few of his friends laugh. You feel embarrassed and your feelings are hurt because you thought you had a good relationship with the student. Ten seconds later, the bell rings and he heads out to his bus. Although you didn't hear exactly what the student said, you know he said something rude under his breath. What should you do?

One option you have is to simply forgive and forget. In some situations, this is truly the best thing to do. In the scenario described above, it was the end of the day on a Friday and everyone, including you, was just ready to go home. Is there a chance that the student won't remember what occurred when he comes to school on Monday morning? Is there a chance that that was a battle that is not worth the fight? Is there a chance the student was just trying to impress his friends before he hung out with them later that night? We are not recommending that you just "ignore" serious misbehavior. Instead, we are reminding you that sometimes kids can be mean for a variety of reasons, just like adults can. Not everything students say should be taken personally, and not everything is worth the battle, especially if it is not repetitive behavior. In some cases, forgiving and forgetting is what's best for you and the student. Even if you don't initially want to, sometimes giving students a "no strings attached" fresh start is just what the doctor ordered. If the student comes in and has obviously moved on, it might be best for us to look out the windshield instead of the rearview mirror as well.

Not everything students say should be taken personally, and not everything is worth the battle, especially if it is not repetitive behavior.

A Fresh Start With Accountability

In contrast with the previous example, sometimes students will do things that you simply cannot "forgive and forget." Maybe in that scenario you *did* hear the student, and it ends up he mumbled something very inappropriate under his breath. You think about it all weekend, and you are struggling to let it go. In scenarios like this one, we would recommend that instead of pretending you are okay with what occurred, you take action in regard to what the student did and follow it with something we call a "fresh start."

For example, let's pretend Sierra, a student that you normally have no issues with, was out of her seat over and over and over on Tuesday. You redirected her multiple times by moving her to the class safe seat, sending her to a buddy room, and eventually you needed to get her removed from class altogether. No matter what you tried to do, she tested you over and over again. This caused you to lose the trust you had in her and frankly hurt your relationship. You know that you want to give her a "fresh start" tomorrow, but you also know that you need to take some type of action to address her misbehavior.

When she walks in the next morning, you choose to have a conversation with her about what happened yesterday. "Hey Sierra, I am happy to see you today! Go ahead and put your stuff up and head to the safe seat for the first part of the lesson so you can make sure you stay focused today. If that goes well then you can go sit with your group again. Grab a pencil and your notebook before you sit down." We would recommend saying this quickly, quietly, and confidently, so the student has less of a reason to react in a negative way. Although this could obviously be worded in a different way, it is a good example of holding a student accountable while also giving her a "fresh start" for that day. You do not scold or shame her for how she acted yesterday, but you provided a consequence that will help her be more successful for the new day.

Open Communication

The final tool we want to give you is to communicate with the student that he or she has hurt your feelings. As you all know, even though our main job is to help students learn content, we also should not be afraid to help students learn "soft skills" as well, like how to communicate or work with people. Most students come to school and give us their best selves (even though it may not always seem like it). However, their "best selves" may still be hard to handle at times. Although we always want to give students patience and understanding, sometimes within that also comes guidance.

For example, let's say that you worked really hard on a study guide for the big test coming up, and you even gave students an entire day to review the study guide to prepare for the test. What a gift! You walk around the classroom to see if anyone has any questions, and you come across a group of kids who are doing everything *but* looking at the study guide. You explain again how to use the study guide and even work through the first problem with these students to help get them back on track, and then you continue monitoring the classroom. About five minutes later, you go back to this group and they have not done one ounce of work since you walked away from them previously. You decide to make them work independently in hopes that they will stay more focused. As you walk away, you hear a student say to their friend, "This is so stupid. I hate this class." Normally you ignore sidebar comments like this, but you had worked *so* hard on this study guide and you had even strayed from the pacing guide to give them this extra day of practice. Your feelings are hurt and you can tell it has made you angry.

In a moment like this, one option you could use is to go to that student and privately tell them how their comment made you feel. Although you can never guarantee how the student will respond, we have found that most students see where the teacher is coming from if the communication is sincere, private, and respectful. One way of responding to the student could be, "I heard what you said, and it honestly frustrated me. I worked so hard the past few days on this study guide because I care about your learning. I also purposefully gave you this full day to work on it just in case you had any questions for me about the material. I understand you may not love school every moment of every day, but what you said did hurt my feelings because I put a lot of effort into this and I really like you as a student." In this scenario, this student probably didn't realize how much time this study guide took and how much you care about them doing well in your class. There is a good chance they really just care about the latest online game they found. Thus, by communicating this and teaching them to think about others, you are repairing the relationship while also teaching them empathy.

You Broke the Relationship. Now What?

You snapped at a student. You yelled at a class. Your lesson crashed and burned. We as teachers are not perfect, it happens. However, when you mess up, are you willing to be vulnerable with your students and admit it? Are you willing to step out of your comfort zone in order to repair for the sake of your relationships? If you are the one who broke the relationship, there is only one way to fix it and the solution requires you to allow yourself to be uncomfortable and vulnerable. This is something a lot of us are afraid to do because we feel we are the authority. We believe that we cannot look weak or admit mistakes or allow defeat. However, we have to keep kids on our side. If you yelled, that was wrong. If your lesson crashed and burned, you let your kids down, that was a mistake. If you break a relationship with a student or an entire class for whatever reason, you must apologize, plain and simple.

As practicing teachers, we realize this is easier said than done. Apologizing sounds like a simple enough fix until you really think about what you are about to embark upon. Do I really have to stand up in front of my entire class and say, . . .

"Sorry, I made a mistake."
"Sorry, I messed up."
"Sorry, I wasn't prepared."
"Sorry, I was really mean."
"Sorry, I lost control of myself."

But the answer is yes, you absolutely do. We are teachers. What better way to teach our students how to apologize than by modeling it ourselves? Students make mistakes all the time and we expect them to apologize. Why should we be held to a lower standard? If a kid yells at you, you *expect* a sorry from them at some point. If you yell at a kid, they *deserve* an apology from you, no matter what. The apology does not have to come that moment, or that class period, or that day. But it should come. Remember that the best way to get in the last word is to apologize.

Below, Katherine has shared a personal story to show how powerful apologizing can be:

I apologized my second year of teaching and have done it a million times since. However, I am now in my 6th year of teaching and you know what? I still get nervous doing it! Being vulnerable is so scary yet so worth it. When thinking back to that first time I apologized, I still get nervous. It was November of my second year of teaching and I was struggling with classroom management. My homeroom was behaving worse than normal during what was supposed to be participating in sustained silent reading. I had allowed students to sit wherever they wanted which ended up being 10 kids piled in a corner of my room doing anything but reading. I could not take the distractions anymore. I was attempting to model good behavior by sitting at my desk and reading, but their actions had gotten so out of control that I couldn't even focus anymore. One day I lost it, "Everyone, back to your seats! This is supposed to be quiet and I can't take it anymore. I am trying to read, we are all supposed to be trying to read, but it has gotten to the point where no one is or can." After that occurred my gut told me I had handled my homeroom incorrectly. I left school with a pit in my stomach knowing I needed to change something.

The next day they all walked back into homeroom and took a seat. I was so nervous. Shaking just like the day before, but this time it was not out of anger. It was out of fear. The bell rang and I began, "Guys, I am so sorry for yesterday. I am sorry that I lost my cool with you. I am sorry I did not make this reading time more structured for everyone. I am sorry that out of frustration I then yelled at you all. I messed up yesterday and take full responsibility. Can we try again today?" Immediately one of my students raised her hand, "Yeah, Jaliyah?" She responded, "Ms. Whitaker, I have never had a teacher apologize to a class before." There were murmurings all around the room in agreeance with what she had said. Although their behavior was unacceptable, much of it stemmed from my lack of effectiveness. My apology allowed myself and the entire class a fresh start, and ever since that moment I was able to slowly but surely improve my management and craft to become the teacher I am today. This shows the power of an apology, the power of being vulnerable, and the power of repairing. Remember that apologizing can make you stronger, not weaker.

Final Thought: Holding Grudges

Whether you choose to repair a relationship by forgiving and forgetting, giving students a fresh start with accountability, or communicating your feelings, one thing that will derail each of these techniques is by holding a grudge. The grudge takes the wind out of whatever sails were built from your attempt at repairing and rebuilding the relationship. Your students will hold grudges. Your colleagues and bosses may even hold grudges. But you will be the exception. You will be the one who knows how to repair and move on.

You will be the one who knows how to repair and move on.

Remember: we are dealing with small children or adolescents. They absolutely, without a doubt, will mess up. That is almost a teaching guarantee, and should probably be included in your teaching contract to remind you of what you are signing up for! Even with that assurance, you should not, for any reason, under any circumstance, hold a grudge against your students. There are no ifs, ands, or buts. The grudge is a relationship crusher, not a repairer. In every situation in a classroom, there needs to be a least one adult and it often works best if that adult is the teacher.

Tweak

As mentioned in chapter 1, you will always need to make small adjustments, or tweaks, to aspects of your classroom throughout the school year. Sometimes, those tweaks will need to be made to relationships you have or have not built with your students. We want to share three common scenarios that teachers find themselves in, and we want to help you see when tweaks need to be made and what adjustments could be made to improve your relationships with your students.

Scenario 1: You Have Great Relationships With Some Students, and Not-so-great Relationships With Others

Every year, most teachers will have students that they instantly connect with. Those relationships are generally built with ease. On the flip side, you will also generally have students that you do not instantly connect with. In fact, you may find yourself four months into the school year still not having formed a bond with those students. So what do you do?

If you struggle to connect with a student or group of students simply because your personalities clash or their maturity level tests your patience regularly, we recommend that you heavily rely on being kind to keep that relationship strong. Sometimes personalities clash, and that's just part of the reality of being human. With that being said, everyone deserves to be treated with respect by their teacher. They may not be your closest students that year and that is okay. As long as you always treat them with kindness and respect, you have done your job.

We would also recommend using the tips we described to show students that you are interested in their lives. In "Part I: Building Relationships," we recommend that you choose 1–2 students each day to make a personal connection with. If you find yourself struggling to connect with certain students, choose them as your focus for the next few days or weeks. This can help you bond with those students that were not instantly drawn to you or your class.

Scenario 2: Instead of Focusing on Being a Teacher, You Focus on Being a Friend

There are also situations that occur where the line between teacher and friend has been blurred. In these situations, teachers are generally too focused on building relationships with students, and not concerned enough with actually teaching students. Or they are nervous to hold students to a certain expectation for fear that they will no longer be liked. This is detrimental for a variety of reasons. First, this impacts student learning, which is the main aspect of our job description. We all went into teaching for a variety of reasons, but one of them needs to be to make sure students learn every single day in our classrooms. If building relationships is preventing that from happening, priorities need to be reassessed. Additionally, becoming lax on expectations and guidelines in hopes that you can become closer to your students not only prevents you from doing your job, it can actually cause the opposite effect: your relationships are eventually hurt because of it.

Think of it this way: let's say that you decided that you should forgo instruction for a day and make that day a "flexible work day." During this time, you hung out with a group of students, talked about music and YouTube videos they like, and felt good about the bonds you built as they walked out of the classroom. Over the next few weeks you did this a few more times until you realized that you need them to take a unit test before the end of the semester. While you are having them do the review activity, they seem to just want to chat and hang out with you. You realize this is a high-stakes test that will significantly impact their grade. You become frustrated that they aren't taking it seriously, and you slowly realize that there are multiple questions on the review that they have no idea how to answer. By the end of the lesson you find yourself on the verge of (or actually) yelling at students while you simultaneously feel like a failure for not teaching them as best as you could have. You know you either can have them take the test and do terribly on it, or hold them to lower expectations by making the test easier. It's a lose-lose situation you've found yourself in, and now your students are mad because you are suddenly no longer the "cool" teacher.

If you think that you may have blurred the line between teacher and friend, we recommend that you fix that as soon as you can. That does not mean that you need to start being mean or never talk to students about things other than school. Instead, it just means that you look to yourself to see what improvements need to be made to rebuild the boundaries and expectations that need to be in place for students to be able to learn in your classroom. Go back into your business-mode by utilizing the first five minutes of each class effectively (as mentioned in chapter 2), holding students to high and clear behavioral and academic expectations (as will be discussed in chapter 4), and not letting yourself "slip" throughout the rest of the year (as will be discussed in chapter 5). You may not even need to make an announcement to the students about the changes you want to make. What is most important is the internal shift to a business mindset. Finally, remember that relationships do not change in one day, so it will take commitment to get your classroom culture readjusted.

Scenario 3: You Assume You Have Good Relationships With All Students, but Their Consistent Rude, Defiant, or Apathetic Behavior Contradicts What You Believe

Some teachers know how to build relationships with students, yet still struggle with rude, defiant, or apathetic behavior. This is a reality for all teachers, even the ones with the best relationships. If you find that this is a persistent issue with large groups of students, however, it may not just be because "kids will be kids." Instead, there could be ways that you are perpetuating this issue, even if you are well intentioned.

This scenario happens in classrooms because some teachers may not realize how they come across to students. You can think that you are being kind or funny, but in reality students see that you are insincere or lacing your words with sarcasm. Being inauthentic with students may cause them to build up walls, become indifferent to your class, or even lash out. If this may be you, we challenge you to analyze what mindset you bring to your classroom, or even ask a trusted yet honest friend who would be straight-forward with you on how you come across to others. You could even record yourself during a lesson or classroom activity and see if things you say or do could be perceived in less-than-appealing ways.

Other times, this occurs because the teacher is not consistently kind or caring. It may seem unfair, but many times one negative comment or action can carry much more significant weight than multiple positive ones. Just think if your principal treated you with respect most of the time, but every now and then he or she lashed out in the middle of a stressful moment. There is a chance that eventually those moments would take a toll on your perception of your principal and even how you feel coming to work. Those negative moments could slowly take over the many positive ones. The same goes for your students. Even if you are nice most of the time, if you have "bad moments" too often and do not repair when they occur, students will potentially begin to disconnect from you and your class.

Lastly, this also may occur because of something other than your behavior: your instruction. As we noted previously, one way to build relationships is to help students be successful in class. Sometimes the actual assignments that are given to students are poorly organized, unclear, or poorly scaffolded, which can cause even the best students to become exasperated or apathetic. If students go into a classroom where they consistently are unable to do the work, many will become rude, defiant, or apathetic in response to their frustration. Even teachers who are consistently friendly can have this issue because most students want to feel successful in school, as we mentioned before. We hope you did not read this and then instantly think that you need to make your lessons or expectations easier to prevent misbehavior. That is the opposite of what we want you to do. Instead, make sure that your lessons and assignments are organized, clear, and scaffolded so students can feel success. Sometimes it can be difficult to give yourself an objective viewpoint about your lessons, so feel free to ask a trusted and honest colleague his or her opinion, or even better yet, ask your students. More often than not, they will be able to give you guidance on what may need to be adjusted.

✅ What You Can Do Tomorrow

1. **Purposeful Interactions.** Choose 1–2 students that you are going to make sure you interact with at some point during the day. Think of the time in your day when you can either say a positive comment to the student or ask him or her a question.
2. **Smile More Often.** Use this as a goal after a particularly rough day or week. Not only can it help you feel better, it can also improve your overall classroom climate.
3. **Provide a Fresh Start.** Was there a negative interaction you had with a student that left you frustrated or hurt? We challenge you to give that student a fresh start, even if accountability needs to be a part of it.
4. **Apologize.** Was there a situation that occurred recently that you knew you could have handled better? Remember that apologizing is always an option when you feel like you crossed a line.

4

The Structure—High and Clear Expectations

Foundational Understanding of the Concept

Now that you have your solid foundation built, we can jump into the "meat and potatoes" of this project: building the actual house! As we had you do previously, we want you to picture your dream house in your head. What would it look like? What style would it be? Would you have any non-negotiables in the floor plan? So let's say that the actual house is being built, but as the process is moving along, you start to notice things are not turning out how you had envisioned. Those weren't the windows you had imagined. You can only seem to find one bathroom, not two like you had hoped for. Eventually, you realize that the builders only put on half of the roof! All of a sudden, the beautiful vision you had has disappeared before your very eyes.

Going back to our house metaphor, the actual structure and look of the house represents the expectations that you hold your students to. We bet that each person reading this has a vision for what they hope their classroom is like every day. There is a chance, however, that when reality hits, students don't seem to behave how you imagined and hoped they would. Just like your house turned out entirely wrong, the same can happen to your classroom culture.

To avoid this, you must have clearly set expectations for two main reasons—you and your students. If your expectations are not clear, it will be difficult for students to follow them. We have all been in situations where we were confused about expectations from our bosses, and the same happens in the classroom with students. We can assume that on the first day of school, most students want to follow the rules, so we have to make sure they are clear enough so students can. Clear expectations mean that they are clear to the students, but that also means they are clear to you. If your expectations are clear, it is much easier to hold students accountable when they are not being followed. As practicing teachers, there have been so many times when we have walked away from a behavior management situation feeling doubt about how well we handled something or if our consequence was fair. Those moments of self-doubt can decrease in number if you know that your students knew what was expected of them in that moment.

* * *

According to Bridget Hamre and Robert Pianta (2006), it is critical for schools and teachers to maintain high behavioral expectations to go along with positive teacher-student relationships. Even if you do not currently work in a setting where these assumptions are school-wide, you are the person who makes expectations in your classroom. If you do not expect kindergarteners to sit quietly during a lesson—then they won't. If you do not expect your 10th graders to stay focused on a task—then they won't. Make sure that you are the teacher that expects your students to behave their best, and explains explicitly what that looks like, so that you and the students know the difference between what is appropriate and what is not.

To discuss this idea, we are going to learn about two teachers, Mr. Johnson and Mrs. Logan, who are 8th grade social studies teachers at the same urban school. They both teach the same curriculum, serve the same clientele, and even use the same procedure where students are allowed to get pencils from the "sharpened pencil" container anytime during the lesson. The outcomes of how each teacher implements the given procedure, however, are strikingly different.

Mr. Johnson came to the team meeting one day frustrated about how many issues he had been having with students getting pencils. Mrs. Logan was surprised at his concerns because she, in fact, loved the procedure they had decided on and was ready to tell the entire school about it at their next faculty meeting. What caused this huge disparity in success? The major differences were the level of expectation for the procedures and how these were communicated to the class.

When Mr. Johnson introduced the procedure, he simply told students that they could get up and get a new pencil at any time. Mrs. Logan also told students that they could get up and get a new pencil at any time, but included that they must do it quietly, and take a specific route behind all of the desks so it will cause as little distraction as possible. That major difference (along with Mrs. Logan's ability to consistently enforce the proper behavior which will be addressed in the next section) was that Mrs. Logan had higher expectations as to how this procedure should be completed. From day one, her students knew that they were entirely free to get pencils whenever they needed them, but they had to do it in a specific way that would prevent any disturbance. Mr. Johnson's students, however, simply knew they could get a pencil at any time. Both classes were following the expectation correctly— but the teachers chose to have different levels of how they expected the procedure to be completed.

Although both teachers had the exact same basic expectation, which classroom culture do you think was more positive and highly functional? This goes back to the idea that many things in education are highly debatable. Mrs. Logan would potentially state that this is the greatest pencil procedure she has ever had, whereas Mr. Johnson may proclaim that this is in fact the worst pencil procedure he has ever implemented. Now you see, however, that in this situation, it isn't the procedure that's "good" or "bad," it's the implementation (or lack thereof) of the high and clear expectations that decides the teacher's level of success.

Personal Reflection—Madeline

During my first year of teaching, one of the most impactful changes I made was to my class's morning routine. By the third day of school, I could tell things needed to change. Students were coming into my classroom in groups from the bus they got off of. This caused them to come in waves full of neighborhood friends. Although I was glad my 3rd graders had camaraderie, I did not like that every morning students brought their friend group "drama" into my classroom. It was throwing off our dynamic every morning without fail, and I knew I needed to do something about it.

Since one of the biggest issues during my morning routine was that students were coming into the classroom in large groups, the first tweak I made was making students line up outside my classroom before they came in. This way, I could greet each student with a smile, which helped build my classroom culture, and I could also control the flow of students into my room, which helped improve my classroom management and protect my sanity. Using this strategy, I let each student go in about every 5 seconds, which prevented the mass chaos that had been occurring previously.

Although things improved significantly, my morning routine still was not exactly what I wanted it to be. Students were now going in individually, but I was struggling to hold them accountable once they actually got inside. I would remind them of my expectations because they seemed to find everything to do other than get their backpacks put away and get started eating breakfast. So the next morning, I still had students line up, but before they would come in, I reminded them of the three things they needed to do every morning: put their items in their cubbies, get their breakfast, and go to their seats.

This really helped the dynamic once students got inside, but I still felt like it was only 85 percent of what I wanted it to be. There were still a few students who were finding loopholes in my expectations. So the next morning, I had the lights turned down before students came in to set a calm tone, and instead of reminding students of what my expectations were, I had them tell *me* what they were. This helped students remember my expectations fully and helped me feel comfortable holding students accountable when they weren't following my directions because I knew that they knew what they should be doing.

The change I made on the final day was having a read aloud playing as students entered one-by-one. All of these small adjustments helped me and my students create a morning routine and classroom culture that we all wanted to be a part of. I hope that this example not only shows the importance of expectations, but also how teachers can choose, adjust, and get rid of ones so their classrooms can be a place that everyone wants to come to.

How-to and Application

Expectations are, in general, what they sound like: what you expect of your students. What do you expect them to do when they walk into your class? How do you expect them to handle cell phones in class? What do you expect them to do when they need a pencil? Expectations provide the much-needed structure for your classroom, and their importance should not be overlooked.

To discuss this, we will dig into two subsets of expectations: rules and procedures/routines. Rules are a teacher's main "non-negotiable" expectations about the behavior and character of a class. A few examples of common rules are: "Complete all assignments," "One person talk at a time," and "Be prepared." Rules generally have

> **Rules are a teacher's main "non-negotiable" expectations about the behavior and character of a class.**

consequences tied to them, because breaking a rule could have a strong effect on the classroom culture. Procedures and routines, on the other hand, are different from rules because they are more narrow, and they generally pertain to specific tasks such as how to get a pencil, how to store classroom technology, the classroom food policy, etc.

As you read about and learn about rules and procedures/routines, we want you to constantly reflect upon the ones you have in your own classroom. We did the exact same thing as we planned, wrote, and edited this book, and we continue to do so every day that we teach. We will never be perfect teachers just as you will never be perfect teachers. We all know, however, that if there are changes that need to be made, adjusting them will not only benefit your students, they will benefit you as well.

Rules

Since we are going to discuss rules first, we want you to think about what rules you currently have or are planning to have in your own classroom. Although this process may seem basic, it is highly important because research shows that establishing clear rules is a critical aspect of successfully managing a classroom (Marzano, Gaddy, Foseid, Foseid, & Marzano, 2005). Some teachers choose to have a set of classroom rules posted on the wall right when students walk in the first day. Some prefer to form the rules together as a class to build student ownership of them. Others may just use the school rules that students are already familiar with, so they only need to be addressed during the first day of class. Some master teachers, especially secondary ones, do not even have explicit rules or expectations posted in their classroom—but they are clearly written in their heads and their students are very aware they exist. *No matter which type of teacher you are, make sure that you have a clear vision of what you are wanting the rules to be.*

Whether you call them rules, expectations, or norms, we want you to think of them as your "non-negotiables." They are the things that you want to consistently happen in your classroom and they are what drives the dynamic of yourself and your students. For some teachers, they even represent their core philosophies of teaching and learning. The key to effective rules is that you know what your non-negotiables are and you know how to communicate them clearly because students must be aware of them. Whenever we walk into new academic situations, one of the first things we want to know is, "What is expected of us?" Is there a chance that students would like to know this too?

Rules are important because, when implemented effectively, they represent the philosophy of the classroom teacher and drive the tone of the classroom. According to Robert Boostrom (1991), they "are structures of meaning we use to make sense of the world around us" (p. 194). Thus, rules not only help create order, but they also are the foundation of your classroom life. Let's go back to the rules you currently have (or hope to have) in your classroom, and see if you can answer "yes" to these questions:

- ◆ Do your rules help create a functional classroom where learning can take place?
- ◆ Are your rules reasonable?
- ◆ Do you feel comfortable consistently enforcing your current classroom rules for all students and over a variety of situations?

If you answered, "No," or, "I'm not sure," to any of those questions, it's time to look at what your current rules are and see if they need to be adjusted or changed. Let's go through these three questions and process examples where a teacher's rules may prevent the students and the classroom flow from being the best they can be.

1. Do your rules help create a functional classroom where learning can take place?

There are two main ways that a teacher's rules can prevent a classroom from running functionally. First, the rules are not clear. As mentioned previously, expectations must be clear or else you really will never know if students are even understanding what they are supposed to do. Sometimes catchy or heart-felt rules like "Be your best self" can seem great at first, but do they really tell students what your non-negotiables are? Could this cause your rule implementation to become inconsistent, since one student's best self is different from someone else's? This is not to say that there are no teachers out there who are successful with ambiguous rules like this one. We feel *very* confident that there are master teachers who could have a highly functional classroom with this as their sole rule because they have a clear internal vision of what this rule looks like and can communicate that to their students. With that said, just because it works for one person doesn't mean it will work for all. There is a chance that making your rules clearer would be beneficial to both you and your students.

So if your rules are not currently helping create a functional classroom where learning can take place, we challenge you to make them slightly more clear. Having issues with students blurting out? Getting out of their seat without asking? Saying hateful things to a classmate? Make sure your rules specifically addresses those issues. "Raise your hand to speak," "Stay in your seat during the lesson," and "Be kind to others" are three basic examples of rules that you could implement. Making these rules will not in themselves stop students from misbehaving in those ways, but having clear guidelines of what is right and what is wrong is the first step to fixing the issue at hand.

2. Are your rules reasonable?

Defining "reasonable" classroom expectations is hard because it can be interpreted in different ways. Let's say that an elementary teacher has a rule where students must whisper during stations, or a secondary teacher has a rule where students cannot take their cell phones out all class period. Some may think that both of these rules are entirely reasonable, while others may believe otherwise. Because reasonableness is such a gray area, instead of giving you examples of expectations that fit along the "reasonableness spectrum," we want to challenge you to think about if your rules are too reasonable, not reasonable enough, or "just right." Many times how you enforce your rules determines the reasonableness as much as the rule itself. Here is a story from one of the authors, Todd Whitaker, about a rule he realized needed an adjustment.

My first year as a teacher I set up a 'rule' that students could not turn in assignments late. Obviously one benefit is that is a clear guideline for all. The students knew that if they did not have the assignment completed when the bell rang to start class they would not get credit for it. NO EXCUSES! If you forgot it, too bad. If you left it at home, too bad. If you left it in your last class, too bad. This seemed reasonable to me. After all, it made it easy for me. No decision making required!

Additionally, I taught math and had classwork and/or homework on a regular basis thus if you did not complete or forgot one assignment it did not matter. No biggie—at least no biggie to me . . . or so I thought.

Then one day we had a major review assignment due. The students had several days of class time to complete it and it was a significant factor on their grade. The day it was due, Tonya, the nicest and most responsible student in the class—whose mother was school secretary and a pleasure to work with—had a very ashen look on her face. She sheepishly raised her hand and said she had left her assignment in her locker and her locker was the closest one in the school to our classroom. Well, a rule is a rule, I thought. The students all looked at me wondering what was coming next. Well, what was coming next was a realization that this was a rule that lacked common sense and more importantly the impact of the consequence on Tonya was ridiculously disproportionate to her misstep. I realized at that point the challenge of thinking you can make black-and-white rules that impact the gray world of teaching.

I announced to the class that my rule was silly in hindsight and that students who had missed previous assignments could turn them in as my focus was on learning the concepts rather than hardlining the rules. From this point forward I had expectations rather than cold hearted rules and it made me a much better teacher. It also helped ensure a strong foundation of positive relationships. And we all need the school secretary on our side!

In this example, we all could see that the rule was preventing students from showing mastery at an unreasonable level for the situation. Changing the rule to a more reasonable expectation allowed Tonya to get her work turned in, and also allowed the other students to do the same. We are not sharing this story to say that what Todd did is exactly what every teacher should be doing. Instead, we share it to show that he realized his rule was unreasonable for his classroom and students, so he changed it.

Sometimes you may need to loosen a rule to make it more reasonable, but we also want to let you know that it is okay to tighten a rule as well. Sometimes teachers can come up with rules that are potentially too reasonable, and they give too much leeway for students to not do what needs to get done, especially if they are overly concerned with students' opinions of themselves or their class. For example, let's say there is a teacher who is okay with students being on their cell phones or classroom devices during direct instruction. This may make the students happy, and they may rave about how "cool" this teacher is, but is there a chance that the technology is preventing their learning? Obviously there is no clear answer because so much depends on the technology used, the students, the age level, etc., but there is a potential that situations like this could be hurting the learning environment.

> **Sometimes you may need to loosen a rule to make it more reasonable, but we also want to let you know that it is okay to tighten a rule as well.**

3. Do you feel comfortable consistently enforcing your current classroom rules for all students and over a variety of situations?

One of the biggest challenges in developing rules is remembering that eventually you will have to enforce them. Thus, it is essential to think through extreme examples in advance to make sure you are comfortable with establishing this guideline. As we mentioned previously, rules are your main "non-negotiables" when it comes to student behavior and character. Whatever rule you put in place, you will have to enforce it on a *consistent* and *daily* basis. Wasicisko and Ross (1994) summarize this idea nicely: "To avoid the pitfalls of inconsistency, mean what you say, and when you say it, follow through" (p. 64). Think about it this way: let's say one of your rules is, "Raise your hand to speak." This rule will strongly support your classroom functionality, but are there ever times you *won't* want students to raise their hand to speak? Do you ever do small group work? Casual class discussions? Partner work? If so, it may be hard to consistently reinforce this rule because your use of this rule may depend on the activity you are having students do that day.

What do you do if you do not feel comfortable consistently enforcing your current classroom rules? You should either eliminate that rule or find a way to adjust it to fit the situation. For example, if you don't want students talking during the lesson, but you do want them to talk during the practice, make your rule specifically state, "Keep voices off during the lesson." This will give you the chance to use the rule in a more effective way by consistently reinforcing it.

* * *

Remember that rules can help provide necessary structure for the teacher and the students. They can be a guideline in order to have consistency and appropriate behavior in the classroom. However, of course, they are not the answer by themselves, just the guardrails within which we operate. Many times as teachers move to a higher level of experience in their careers the number of rules they need may become minimal or be eliminated entirely. One thing to remember is that when we have rules we need to enforce them or we do not really have rules at all, and doing this consistently will be something that will be touched upon in the next chapter. It is one of the many things about teaching that require a deft touch. Thinking through what you need as non-negotiables in your classroom is essential in order to implement effective rules.

Procedure and Routines

When we think of rules, we think of what sets the groundwork to create a highly functional classroom. A teacher's set of rules can almost be viewed as a mission and vision statement for a company. It sets the tone and represents what both students and teachers should strive for every day in that classroom. What about the day-to-day tasks, though? What about when a student simply needs to go to the bathroom? Although that is not something we would focus on in our class mission and vision statement, we all know the mass confusion that would occur if none of your students knew what to do if they had a bathroom emergency. Thus, after you solidify what rules you have in your classroom, you also need to think extensively about classroom procedures and routines.

Procedures are basic routines that you and students will use to help the classroom "run," almost like a well-oiled machine.

Procedures are basic routines that you and students will use to help the classroom "run," almost like a well-oiled machine. Research has shown that procedures are a critical aspect of preventative effective classroom management that positively affect students' learning and behavior (Marzano et al., 2005; Stronge, Tucker, & Ward, 2003). Effective routines are what differentiates teachers who mainly "manage" their class from teachers who mainly "discipline" their class (Lester, Allanson, & Notar, 2017, p. 410). Consequently, thinking deeply about procedures in a proactive manner can be a huge make-or-break with regard to student management and overall classroom climate. The tighter your procedures are, the less misbehavior will occur and the calmer and more productive the environment will be. Listed below are questions that need to be answered by the teacher to ensure that procedures are in place in the classroom:

- ◆ Pencils—How will students get them? How will they get sharpened? What if a student forgets one? What if the student needs an eraser?
- ◆ Notebooks/Textbooks—Will students come into the classroom each day with them? If not, how will you get them handed out each day? What if a student comes one day without them?
- ◆ Assignments/Homework—Where will it be turned in or how will you collect it? How will you return it to the students after grading?

◆ Late work—How will students learn about what information they missed? What system will you use so they have access to the make-up work?

◆ Bathroom—How often can students use the bathroom? How will they let you know that they need to use the bathroom? Will you need to keep track of how many times a student has used the bathroom?

◆ Technology—How will classroom technology be stored? If portable, how will it be distributed to students? Will devices need to be charged overnight?

◆ Phones, tablets, personal devices—What is your school's policy? What is your classroom policy? When are the times students can access them? When are the times they should be put away?

◆ Entering the classroom—Should students remove hats? Are they to be quiet? Should they go straight to their seats? What work should they get started on?

◆ Exiting the classroom—Will you dismiss students? Do they leave when the bell rings? Is there a line order they must learn? Should they line up quietly?

Below we have included an extensive and specific list of possible things that will require procedures in your classroom. Although this may not be an exhaustive list of everything you have an expectation for, we hope either this list or the questions above jog your memory of procedures that you may need to adjust or rethink.

◆ Tissues
◆ Students asking questions
◆ Checking out books from the school library and/or your classroom library
◆ Eating food in the classroom
◆ Taking attendance
◆ Fire drill
◆ Beginning of the day/period routines
◆ End of the day/period routines
◆ Tornado drill

- ◆ Lost items
- ◆ Throwing away trash and/or recycling
- ◆ Storing and distributing materials that may not be used daily (crayons, colored pencils, scissors, glue, etc.)
- ◆ Classroom jobs
- ◆ Unfinished work
- ◆ Technology availability and utilization
- ◆ Earthquake Drill
- ◆ Late work
- ◆ Make-up work
- ◆ Seating arrangement
- ◆ Students who are tardy
- ◆ Acceptable noise levels
- ◆ Talking and participating during lessons
- ◆ Getting into/choosing groups
- ◆ Lockdown Drill
- ◆ Sudden illness
- ◆ Dismissal
- ◆ Restroom visits
- ◆ Sharpening pencils

I've Chosen My Rules and Procedures . . . Now What?

We have now deeply discussed the two basic "tried and true" aspects of classroom management, but what we have touched upon is only half the story. So you have effective rules and thoughtful procedures, but what do you *do* with them? How do you make sure students truly understand them? How do you use them as a catapult to create the classroom culture you want? What we are going to discuss next is where the magic happens. This is where you take those rules and procedures and turn them into culture-driving tools. This is where you make sure that your expectations, whether they are rules or procedures, are clearly explained and reinforced.

Whether you are teaching 1st grade or 11th grade, you must let your students know how to complete whatever task you are asking them to do. We want to share a flow that you can use when introducing any structures in your classroom. This list can and should be adjusted based on the grade level that you teach.

Preschoolers and kindergarteners will most likely need all of these steps, possibly more than once. On the other hand, seniors in high school will most likely only need one or two of these steps before they will catch on. The one thing we want you to remember is that it is always easier to start out with tight structures and get more lax than to do the reverse, and it is easier to hold students accountable for misbehavior when you are confident that they understand what is expected of them. Thus, do not be afraid to do more than just step 1 of the recommendations. We would rather have you be unnecessarily clear than end up with students who become defiant because they didn't understand what was expected of them in the first place.

Below are the five steps we recommend you to take to make expectations as clear as possible. Generally, elementary classrooms flourish when all steps are followed and repeated multiple times, while secondary classrooms can find success using just steps 1–2, and 3 when needed.

1. Clearly explain the task you want students to complete.
2. Physically and verbally model how you want it completed.
3. Have a few students model or explain how you want it completed.
4. Have the task completed in small groups (may be skipped depending on the task and the students' level of independence).
5. Have the task completed as a whole class (after success).

Note: If students are not successful with one step, repeat that step until you find success.

In this flow, we start out being extremely explicit with what we expected through our words and actions. Once we felt like it had been explained well enough, we then had one or two students model or explain it themselves. We do this to make sure that students are understanding what is being asked of them while also giving the students not modeling a chance to see it done well again. As students are modeling or explaining, it is important to point out the things that students are doing well. If a student does or explains something incorrectly, you should ask the student to do it again after either you or other classmates correct the mistake in a gentle manner. For example, "I love how Jennie quietly walked over to her locker. Jennie, can I actually have you do it one more time walking the other way around the room? I think that may help with traffic flow when pack-up time is actually going on." The teacher did not criticize what Jennie did, but instead had her do it again while explaining why and emphasizing that is how it should be done from now on. After that, we had students complete it in small groups, and then if students have done it successfully in small groups for a few days, you could then have the entire class do it at the same time (although this should only be used when you feel confident that your whole class can be successful in this looser structure).

You may feel like your students are too old to do steps such as modeling, pointing out what others are doing well, etc. Many secondary teachers incorrectly assume the students inherently know what to do. A challenge is if they do not know the correct way it becomes difficult to build the relationships you desire because you now have to correct students instead of reinforcing them doing the desired procedures. You can trust your instincts on this but remember that it is much more challenging to tighten structures and expectations than it is to loosen them.

* * *

To be sure we are making the concept of high and clear expectations as clear as possible, we have included two detailed examples of teachers that are teaching their students new procedures. As we have said before, these are not going to be a specific blueprint that will perfectly match your classroom and your students. Instead, we hope you can read them and take from them the most helpful parts that will give you the tools to be as clear about your expectations as possible.

In Ms. Smith's 2nd grade classroom, students are learning how to appropriately line up in line order. She had the line order posted on the board, and she explained the task she needed her students to complete clearly. "Class, right now, since we are about to head to lunch, we are going to practice lining up at the door. When we line up, we calmly stand out of our seats, push our chairs in, and quietly walk to our line spot. I am going to show you how to do it." Ms. Smith models it, and then asks students to point out things that she did that made it a successful transition. After this, she continues, "Now that you have seen what it looks like to line up in my classroom, can I have a volunteer model this for everyone? Thank you for raising your hand Devonte. Can you show the class how a 2nd grader should line up?" While Devonte is modeling this, Ms. Smith points out all of the things that she likes that Devonte is doing. "Wow, notice how Devonte considerately pushed in his chair, and calmly walked to the line. Also, he was so quiet I don't think I heard his shoes tap the ground!" After Devonte returns to his seat, Ms. Smith asks for another volunteer, and this time she asks the *students* to point out things that the new student is doing well while transitioning. Finally, Ms. Smith wants to release the students in table groups, but before she does, this is how she sets up her students for success, "Now that I see what incredible students I have in my class, I can tell we are ready to get lined up for lunch! Don't forget—I am looking for students who calmly stand out of your seat, push your chair in, and quietly line up. Which table group thinks they can do this the best?" Ms. Smith will then dismiss each table group until everyone is lined up.

This example is perfect for young students who need extremely tight structures and explanations. What about older students, or ones who may not need such repetition, and who may have more extensive instructions to follow? In Ms. Logan's 8th grade social studies class, she is teaching students how they will need to grade and turn in their bellringer each day. "Every day you will come into class with a bellringer, or a task to do right when you enter the classroom, on the board. The expectations for this task will always be hung above the door, and you will have five minutes to complete it." As Ms. Logan continues to explain the procedure, she is walking around and modeling each step. While doing this, she refers to the list of steps she has displayed on the board. "If you complete the bellringer before the five-minute timer goes off, I will want you to check one of the answer sheets I will have face down on the table in the front of the room. If you get it correct, you can turn your bellringer into the homework bin, and if you get it incorrect you can head back to your seat and explain why you had the misconception that you did on your paper with a pen. When you have turned it in, you can sit quietly at your seat and read or work on homework. Once the five-minute timer goes off, I will then collect all of the papers."

Ms. Logan realizes that she shared a lot of steps in that explanation, so she knows it is crucial to ask students to reiterate what she had just explained. "Can someone tell me in their own words what you do if you finish before the five-minute timer goes off?" If students can successfully explain this, she can continue to ask about each of the different steps. If students cannot, then she will re-explain and model the steps again herself before asking them to explain it again. Before she has a student model the procedure, she reiterates her high expectations. "Class, I have one final, critically important part of our procedure: it must be silent the entire time because most of our bellringers will be independent work, and I want everyone to be able to concentrate as much as possible without distraction." Now she knows that the class is ready for a faux bellringer practice session. First, she has one or two students model what it looks like to check their work and then return to their seat. She decides to skip the 4th step of having the task completed using small groups because she feels comfortable with the level of independence her students have shown.

During the whole-class practice session, Ms. Logan is walking around, quietly pointing out things that students are doing well, while also redirecting students who have forgotten the steps. "Sarah you grade in purple pen!? That's awesome, I wish I had one." "Jacoby your handwriting is better than mine. Thank you for making your work so neat and organized." "Tyler you got done so quickly. I appreciate you moving onto reading when you were done. What book are you reading? Is it good?" Notice how Ms. Logan is reinforcing the behavior she is looking for, but in a more discreet way. Instead of saying outright, "Sarah, thank you for grading your paper in pen," Ms. Logan makes a comment that aims at building a relationship while still emphasizing the behavior she is looking for. In this type of interaction, she uses her knowledge about the type of feedback her students best respond to, and then applies it directly to the situation.

After the five-minute timer goes off and she has collected the bellringers, she then has students give feedback as to what went well and what could improve for next time. This helps improve student buy-in and clarity because now both the teacher *and* the students are thinking through all of the steps for the task. The feedback could be on what went well as a whole class or what the specific student liked about the activity. "Everyone in the room was so quiet!" "I liked that I could rework and make corrections to my problem in pen." The feedback could also be about what changes could be made for next time, whether it's something the teacher needs to do differently or something the students need to do differently. "Do you think it would be better if we all took the same path up to the answer key so people do not bump into each other?" "Should there be more than one answer key, and if so, is there a better place for them to be placed?" Although some of the students were successful with this bellringer, there were a few that were not. Thus, Ms. Logan decides to try it again with a different problem to make sure that every student knows exactly what is expected. "All of your feedback was right on target. I have another great brain-busting question ready so we can practice this procedure one more time. I want this to be streamlined so we are ready for the real thing tomorrow!"

High Expectations for Yourself

As a teacher, we expect a certain level of effort, respect, and work ethic from our students. We have rules that we ask students to follow. We have deadlines we ask them to meet. We have assignments and assessments we expect them to complete. And we get frustrated when students do not follow those expectations. We all have been in this scenario at some point in our career. One thing that is interesting though, is how some teachers get frustrated when students don't live up to expectations, yet those teachers don't hold themselves to the same level of performance. They spend time complaining about how this student didn't get his work turned in last week or how that student was rude during last week's lesson. Yet, that same teacher sends out a hateful email to other staff members, or is on his or her cell phone during an important professional development.

We are not here to be the "teacher police" and claim that all teachers need to behave perfectly all of the time. We are teachers and we sure don't live up to that standard! Teachers do not need to be perfect. Teachers do not need to happily accept every duty that is put on our plate. Teachers do not need to pretend to be happy when things are not going well. With that said, we need to try our best to live and teach with integrity. If we expect students to listen while someone is talking, we should do the same. If we expect students to be respectful even when they are angry, we should do the same. If we expect students to try their best in class every day, we should do the same. So what does that look like in the classroom? We have an example to explain what we are talking about.

Mrs. Jeffery prohibits cell phone use during class until the last five minutes. She follows the school's policy that says if a student has his or her cell phone out without the teacher's permission, it gets taken by the teacher, no questions asked. The phone is then sent to the office and a parent or guardian must come retrieve the cell phone for the student. One day, Abraham's cell phone goes off in class and Mrs. Jeffery follows school policy. She is being consistent and fair, which is obviously a quality of effective classroom managers. Although Abraham may be unhappy, it's school policy and he knows it's what the teachers have to do. Over the next few weeks, Mrs. Jeffery started to set her cell phone on her desk. She did this for emergencies since she has two young kids in daycare, and she wants to have it available just in case a crisis occurs. Fair enough. As time goes on, however, she starts to text regularly while students are in class. No longer does she save it for emergencies. Instead, she is texting friends, colleagues, and is even scrolling through her social media accounts while students are working. Although this may not be a huge issue for some students and classes, it is obvious that Mrs. Jeffery is not holding herself to the same standard that she is holding her students.

We are not saying that teachers must do everything exactly as their students do. That obviously should not be the case because teachers are in charge of students and have authority over them. With that said, we must hold ourselves to a high standard because we are professionals. We are the example in our classrooms. We show students how to behave and what kind of effort should be put forth. If you consistently sit at your desk behind your laptop for the

> **With that said, we must hold ourselves to a high standard because we are professionals. We are the example in our classrooms.**

majority of the class or subject block, what message is that sending to students and how is it improving your classroom environment? If you expect your students to be working all hour on the task at hand, shouldn't you be doing that as well?

All we ask is for you to be the best you can be. We want to emphasize the *can* in that sentence because there are going to be days that you just can't. Trust us, we get it. What we ask of you is that your *can* days significantly outnumber your *can't* days. Be aware of how many *can't* days you are having. Too many, and you are hurting your students, your school, and yourself. And when it comes to your *can't* days, you avoid the behaviors that chip away at your integrity as a professional. We do not expect you to be perfect every day. All we are saying is be the best you possibly can be each and every day. It's what you should expect of your students and it's what you should expect of yourself.

Tweak

Throughout your teaching career, you will find yourself tweaking rules and expectations that you swore would serve you well for years to come. Technology develops, students change, school policies shift, and maybe even your entire job description evolves. Whatever the case, we want to make sure you feel comfortable making changes when they need to be made. Although choosing your rules and procedures and sticking with them from day one can be beneficial, sometimes they do need to be changed or adjusted because life happens. To give you an idea of tweaks that can be made to improve your expectations, Katherine and Madeline have provided an annotated version of the procedures that were shared previously. In this list, they share procedures they currently feel good about, adjustments they have made to improve others, and even share about how they are still searching for the right solution to some particularly difficult ones. We hope that this insight from them will help you feel comfortable celebrating your own successes while also acknowledging what could still be improved.

◆ Facial Tissues—**Madeline: "When I taught 3rd grade, I felt like I had such a solid routine. Students would use a hand signal to let me know they needed a tissue, and I would let them do so. When I moved to 8th grade, however, I realized quickly that asking to get a Kleenex (and even hand-sanitizer) was actually a code word for 'I want to spend 10 minutes walking to the Kleenex box so I can talk to my friends and then spend 10 minutes walking back to get as many students off task as possible.' I now know that in some classes I can let students get their own Kleenexes, while in others I need to bring the box to the student."**

◆ Students asking questions

◆ Checking out books from the school library and/or your classroom library—**Madeline: "Lesson learned from my first year of teaching:** *Don't let students use the 'Property of Ms. Whitaker' stamp without supervision."*

◆ Eating food in the classroom—**Madeline: "I try to be understanding about snacks and drinks, but I have also learned that students like sharing snacks and drinks, which is where the issues get started in my classroom. So although I am okay with students snacking while they are doing independent work, sharing during class is definitely not an option."**

◆ Taking attendance—**Katherine: "After 5 years I still can't quite figure this one out! Some days I'm tricked into thinking I have it down. My kids are quietly working on their warm-up and I can take attendance with ease. Other days they come in like a tornado and I forget to take attendance until lunch . . ."**

◆ Fire drill

◆ Beginning of the day/period routines—**Madeline: "Feel great about this! Yay for a teacher-win!" Katherine: "HELP ME!"**

◆ End of the day/period routines—**Katherine: "I love my end-of-period routine. I let my kids know when they have two minutes left and they get started packing up. They know to put calculators away and return borrowed pencils. I do not let anyone go until my room is looking like how it started."** Madeline: **"When I taught 3rd grade, I was never able to perfect my end-of-the-day routine. It always felt overwhelming and stressful, even when it was structured. If I ever teach elementary again, I will need to try something different for sure."**

◆ Tornado drill

◆ Lost items—**Katherine: "I have a pile on top of a cabinet of things students leave in my classroom. Nothing ever gets taken from it so it just gets worse throughout the year. I need to figure out where the school lost and found is located . . ."**

◆ Throwing away trash and/or recycling

◆ Storing and distributing materials that may not be used daily (crayons, colored pencils, scissors, glue, etc.)—**Madeline: "I currently need to make markers more accessible/replace the bag they are in because it's been poked through one too many times."** Katherine: **"I need new baskets for my dry erase markers and erasers. They are wicker and starting to break after 5 years of consistent use."**

◆ Classroom jobs

◆ Unfinished work—**Katherine: "I have these awesome six pocket folders I use for each class. I recollect work every day (completed or not) for my students because they tend to lose things. These folders are a lifesaver!"**

◆ Technology availability and utilization—**Katherine: "My school is one-to-one and most kids have cell phones. Reminding students to put electronics away before/during notes every day is so frustrating! Need to think about ways to fix this issue."** Madeline: **"When I started teaching 8th grade, cell phones quickly became the bane of my existence. After reaching out to teachers at other schools, I learned about a management idea called 'cell phone jail' where students must put their cell phones in manila envelopes if they are excessively on them at inappropriate** times or if I have asked them to put them away already. It has been such a lifesaver, and some students even ask to put their phones in 'jail' at the beginning of class to prevent themselves from being on them for too long!"

◆ Earthquake Drill

◆ Late work—**Katherine: "I always tell kids to just put it on my desk. Not a great plan."**

◆ Make-up work—**Katherine: "Still struggling to figure out what participation work I should require students to complete if they miss and when they would get it done. If it was a class activity, what do you do?"** Madeline: **"Every day students are given a participation grade and a grade on a 1–2 question exit ticket over that day's content. When students are gone, I just make them exempt from a participation grade for that day and only require them to make up the exit ticket. This helps cut down on confusion regarding make-up work in my classroom."**

◆ Seating arrangement

◆ Students who are tardy

◆ Acceptable noise levels—**Madeline: "One of my favorite things to do with my 3rd graders was to practice whispering during the first month of school. I wanted to let my students talk during reading, writing, and math workshop, but if their voices would get louder than a whisper while I was teaching a small group, my head would begin to spin backwards. Training them to whisper gave them a chance to talk while also making sure I could teach my lessons effectively."**

◆ Talking and participating during lessons—**Katherine: "I expect students to participate because I use a cold calling technique. I love it because it keeps my students on their toes and lets me know how they are each grasping the material."**

◆ Getting into/choosing groups—**Katherine: "I find that I have to adjust this year-by-year or even class-by-class. My kids this year HATE working in groups, whether they get to pick them or I do. They always prefer to work alone. So when we do group activities this year, I have** had to choose them all on my own. In previous years I have been able to sometimes choose them on my own or sometimes let them choose depending on each class's dynamic."

◆ Lockdown Drill
◆ Sudden illness
◆ Dismissal
◆ Restroom visits
◆ Sharpening pencils—**Madeline: "When I taught 3rd grade I had students hold up a fist if they ever needed a pencil, and hold their pencil in a fist if they ever needed their pencil sharpened. If they needed a pencil sharpened, I would grab it, sharpen it quickly, and then return it to the student. This worked out very well with my class because we didn't have to exchange any words for me to know what my students needed."**

What You Can Do Tomorrow

1. **Adjust Classroom Rules**. After reading this section, did you think of any classroom rules that need to be tweaked? Do you have any rules that you are not able to hold students accountable to? Are you missing a rule that could help tighten up your classroom flow?

2. **Change Procedures**. Have you thought of any procedures that need to be adjusted or added to your management system? Maybe your cell phone policy is not working, or students have been loudly sharpening pencils in the middle of your lesson? Feel free to change or add a procedure for tomorrow to see if it can help fix the problem.

3. **Explain Procedures**. Are there any procedures you have that need to be explained again or are you planning to teach procedures in the next few weeks? Look through the five-step process we provided and decide what your students will need to learn the new procedure. Remember that over-explaining will generally be a better mistake to make than under-explaining.

4. **Check Your Personal Expectations**. Have there been any times you have let yourself become possibly too relaxed in regard to personal expectations? Have you avoided interacting with students? Been on your device frequently during class? Thrown together last-minute lessons that probably could have been better with a little more thought? We do not think teachers need to be superheroes, but since we are all human, it can sometimes be easy to let things slide "just once" before you quickly turn it into a bad habit. Think about one way that you may have let yourself get used to some not-so-good habits, and choose one adjustment you want to make tomorrow to rise to the expectations you know you should reach for.

5

The Maintenance—Consistency

Foundational Understanding of the Concept

Congratulations! You have now completed your entire house. You have a sturdy foundation that holds your new house. Your high and clear expectations helped you get the house of your dreams, and you are so happy to now be living in it. One day, while still in your "new house bliss," you go upstairs and hear your bathroom faucet leaking. It is just a slow drip, so you don't think anything of it. A few weeks go by, and you realize the leak has gotten progressively worse. You promise yourself that you will call a plumber the next chance you get. Life got a bit crazy which made it harder for you to find time to call the plumber, but you weren't worried because you knew that the leak would be fine. It's just a small leak, right? Well, it's a small leak until you walk into your living room after a weekend away and you have a water spot in the ceiling from the leak upstairs. Although it started as a small leak, since it wasn't taken care of, it turned into a big problem.

Let's take a look at an example regarding the connectivity between consistency and high expectations for your students. Mr. Kendrick is a middle school social studies teacher. He takes his job, and student learning very seriously. He teaches a lesson and assigns homework on the very first day of school to set a precedent for how 7th grade social studies is going to look this year. Students know that they will be learning every single day because that is the expectation Mr. Kendrick set up. The first week in October Mr. Kendrick is starting to get a little worn out, so on a Friday he decides to spice things up and shows a couple of funny YouTube videos to start class. Students love it and come back on Monday begging for more YouTube videos. Mr. Kendrick declines their requests and they have a solid week of learning. That next week, however, Mr. Kendrick had just finished up a unit and decided a day off of learning could be fun for students. He lets them have a free period to reward them for good work. The next day students come in begging for another free day. Mr. Kendrick allowed them 10 minutes of free time because, why not? His students are great and it won't hurt anything. However, 10 minutes turns into 13 because redirecting them after free time is harder than Mr. Kendrick expected.

As the week continues, students keep asking for bits of free time or clips of YouTube videos. Mr. Kendrick agrees to their requests here and there depending on the day, no harm no foul. As the month progresses Mr. Kendrick realizes a difficult unit is coming up and knows it is time to buckle down and focus. He comes in on Monday with a great lesson ready to go, yet his students are begging for YouTube. Begging for free time. Begging for anything but learning. Mr. Kendrick's expectation of learning social studies every day has been broken. Now, it can be fixed, but he is going to have to work to regain that atmosphere within his classroom. His consistent expectation of learning was broken in only a few weeks. He had good intentions and we can all relate to that 'tired' feeling, but you have to be aware of the repercussions of repeated inconsistencies.

That leaky faucet ended up causing a major water stain because of one thing: you forgot the importance of maintaining your house. You can have the most solid foundation and the perfect structure/design, but if you forget that you must maintain what has been created, your hard work will eventually be for naught. The same can be seen in the classroom example. Loosening up your expectations caused a bad day, and this was because of one thing: you forgot the importance of consistency. When thinking in the context of classroom management, you can have the greatest student relationships and thoughtful high and clear expectations, but if you do not consistently reinforce those relationships and expectations, your whole classroom management system can crumble.

We don't use these examples to shame anyone for avoiding calling the plumber or loosening your classroom expectations. *We have all done it.* The problem is, if it occurs too often, small problems can slowly grow. In situations like these, students typically do not leap from ideal behavior directly to an out-of-control action. It is much more likely that students make a subtle step-by-step slide downward that was allowed to occur. Not only does lack of consistency hurt your ability to teach and students to learn, even more concerningly, it can kill your classroom culture. Research has shown that inconsistent procedures "destabilize students," which kills classroom climate and prevents learning from taking place (Lacourse, 2011, p. 78). As we mentioned previously, the way to make your rules and procedures a part of your positive classroom environment is by implementing high and clear expectations *with consistency*. When you lose this critical third piece, you chip away at your culture until it becomes muddled for both you and your students.

> **As we mentioned previously, the way to make your rules and procedures a part of your positive classroom environment is by implementing high and clear expectations *with consistency*.**

So what could we have done differently to prevent this from occurring? Potentially you could have chosen to not "loosen the reins" in the first place. Or you could have explicitly told students that even though this is what you are doing today, tomorrow it will be back to normal. You could even have pre-scheduled days where both you and your students know that your general expectations will be different because you are having them do a different task. No matter what you do, this can never be the "norm," and students need to know that. You need to be consistent about your high and clear expectations so days where you may be more relaxed are few and far between, and when they do occur, you and your students know that this is not how it will be the next day. We are not saying you can never relax your consistency, but if you choose to, it needs to be very carefully thought through and implemented in a way that protects your classroom functionality and culture.

As a final thought, we realize that most of you probably have students with IEPs (Individualized Education Program) and 504 plans in your classrooms. Even with this diversity, you can still have basic classroom procedures and expectations that all students must follow, but you may have to change them based on those students' capabilities. In situations like these, fair is not always equal, but you must have some structures in place to make sure that you can have a manageable classroom that students can succeed in. Also remember that just because a student has an IEP and a 504 does not mean that you can make excuses for him or her. That actually does a disservice to those students because then they get comfortable performing at below their potential. Thus, when planning the necessary adaptations for these students, do not begin to make excuses just because they are in the exceptional education category. Never forget that all students matter and all students have a capacity to learn. Do not let your excuses prevent your students from living up to their full potential.

Personal Reflection—Todd

During my first year as a teacher I had an amazingly consistent student. He slept in every one of his classes every day—including mine. While some of his other teachers may have been glad that he was disengaged and not being disruptive, I felt that my responsibility as an instructor was to get him engaged and attentive in class. I realized that he had been 'disciplined' by teachers his entire life with little or no positive result. It was important for me to come up with a different approach to increase his investment in class.

I thought about it over the weekend and decided that I needed to try and come up with a way to have him—Curtis—connect with class. I taught middle school math and regularly called on kids throughout my lessons regardless of whether or not they raised their hands. I realized that I could use this aspect of my instruction to hook Curtis in.

Curtis came into class on Monday and I shared that I needed his assistance. He was wary at first, but I explained that I was a new teacher and needed some help. I told Curtis that one concern I had was calling on students equitably in class, but I was not sure that I was very good at it. Did I call on boys more than girls? Did I call on students from the front of the room more often than those in the back rows? I wanted his help to keep track of patterns that I tended to follow in order to get students participating. I gave him a seating chart and asked him to make marks by each student that I called on so that at the end of class I would be able to see if I involved everyone.

After the class period wrapped up, I excitedly went up to Curtis and inquired, "Did I call on boys or girls the most?" Curtis sheepishly handed me the seating chart and the only mark on it was a puddle of his spittle where he had fallen asleep on the paper.

It would have been easy to surrender or even become angry, but I knew this was not going to help. So the next day I gave him a clean seating chart and asked him to see if I called on the left side of the room or the right side of the room the most. Although he wasn't perfect at that task either, he at least had recorded a few marks. I kept this up every day regardless of how he performed the previous day. Eventually he started getting into it. When I would approach him after class he actually started telling me the amount of boys and girls I had called on. After a couple of weeks I divided the chart into quadrants for him to monitor how evenly I called on students throughout the entire room. I would ask him to use a 'v' when a student was a volunteer with his or her hand raised, and an 'n' for 'non-volunteer': someone I had called on who hadn't raised their hand. My goal was to have him focus even more.

Gradually Curtis started doing ratios, fractions, and per-centages with the data that he was collecting. I knew that I had him hooked when one day he came up and shyly asked, "If I answer questions should I put marks by my name also?" One of the key reasons this eventually impacted Curtis was that I did it consistently. I did not give up after three bad days. Each day I smiled and handed him a new chart. Each day he had a clean slate.

No one expects a teacher to be perfect, but consistency in the classroom is a little like being on a diet. Sometimes we slip up, but if we really want to see a benefit we must get back on course tomorrow. And if we mess up too long it spoils any results that may have previously occurred. Consistency may be the simplest of the three foundational pieces in our house metaphor, but it also may be the most challenging. Having positive relationships with students along with clear, appro-priate expectations is essential, but if we are not consistent in how we handle situations in our classrooms day in and day out, our house will slowly crumble to pieces.

How-to and Application

Managing Yourself

Before we begin to discuss how to manage your students, we want you to know that the number one rule for handling any and every behavior situation is consistently managing yourself. You will notice that in almost every scenario, we will describe how you should be 'calm,' 'firm,' or 'confident.' You can never control

> You can never control every single thing a child does, but you can control every single thing that *you* do.

every single thing a child does, but you can control every single thing that *you* do. Tom and Marsha Savage from Santa Clara University argue why teachers must "respect the dignity of the student" in their book *Successful Classroom Management and Discipline: Teaching Self Control and Responsibility* (2009, p. 131). They say that teachers must "respect the dignity of the student" for two reasons: we have a moral obligation to do so, and it will help prevent students from "striking back" since they will not feel the need to go on the defensive. The way that you as a teacher can prioritize doing this is by managing yourself.

Thus, when you are reading through the different behavior management situations and techniques, always remember that what you do and how you handle it is what will decide if the situation goes well or goes poorly. Though a lot of things can influence how much you can affect student behavior, you have 100 percent influence on your own behavior. Thus that should always be the starting point. Use this section to reflect on your previously held conceptions about student management and behavior, and be prepared to either reinforce or re-evaluate your beliefs about how to manage students. Just remember that it always starts with *you*.

In addition, please never forget that you are the adult in the situation, and thus you must hold yourself to such standards. Adults should not argue, ridicule, or demean when managing behavior. Also, adults should not hold grudges. Just as we hope people forgive us if we make mistakes, students want the same thing. If a student has a bad "moment," you handle the moment in an appropriate way, but then move on. Moving on may take 1 minute if the behavior is minor, or it may take 2 hours if it was a more significant incident. Either way, always remember that every day is a new day, and students need to feel welcome in your class no matter what happened the day before. You are the adult, and you must be the model. So, no arguing, no ridiculing, no demeaning language, and especially, no holding grudges.

Bag of Tricks

Picture this: You have gotten about half of your class into their seats, quietly doing their first task, when you notice your student Kathleen has begun to talk to her classmate Akio. Being quiet during the first task is a non-negotiable in your class, and students know it. This is a test of your consistency. Even if you have a great relationship with Kathleen and she knows your expectations, if you do not consistently reinforce them, your house will crumble. So what do you do?

Every teacher has what we call a "bag of tricks." These are strategies that any teacher can use to improve student misbehavior, from effective ones like proximity to poor ones like yelling or using sarcasm. What's interesting is that both effective and ineffective classroom managers have very similar tricks in their bags, but their classrooms look so strikingly different. Why is this? First, effective classroom managers do not need to pull something out of their bag of tricks as often as ineffective classroom managers. If you have strong relationships, high and clear expectations, and engaging and appropriate lessons, some of the more basic tricks hovering at the top of the bag (e.g., ignoring and using proximity) are generally effective and even unneeded. The more we work to prevent misbehavior, the fewer tricks we will need to rely on.

Ineffective managers, however, have to pull out tricks more regularly, and eventually, you get to the tricks at the bottom of the bag that none of us truly want to use. If you are constantly having to pull tricks out of your bag, you'll find that even the most patient teachers will hit their limit. There is no one thing that always works or we would only have one thing in our bag of tricks. That is how come we need to work to diminish how often we reach in, because eventually we will end up pulling out the ugly ones. Then potentially, all of our work to build relationships can become quite tarnished.

The second major difference between how effective and ineffective classroom managers use their bags of tricks is knowing which ones to choose. As a teacher, you are in the classroom to teach students. Yes, we also do so many other things throughout the day, but in the end, we know we are held accountable for student learning. Thus, we always want to choose tricks that fit into two main categories: they are as non-invasive to the learning environment as possible and they de-escalate the situation. For example, let's pretend you are a 1st grade teacher, and it is silent reading time in your classroom. You notice your

Thus, we always want to choose tricks that fit into two main categories: they are as non-invasive to the learning environment as possible and they de-escalate the situation.

student Nara dozing off into space. Before you choose how to handle the situation, you want to think through what options you have in your bag of tricks. You could curtly say, "Nara, get back on task," but did that response fill in the two main categories? Was it as non-invasive as possible and did it de-escalate the situation? Of course not! Although Nara was wasting time, nobody else noticed and nobody else's learning environment was affected until you jumped in. Instead, you should respond in the least-invasive way possible that will also get Nara back on track. One teacher may choose to try out proximity, while another may choose to ask her if she is enjoying the book she is reading. There is never going to be one "perfect" response to student misbehavior. Just always remember that not every trick is created equal.

Let's circle back to the earlier example where Kathleen is talking during the first task. Now when we ask what you should do, we hope your instincts tell you that however you choose to respond, you need to make sure it's the least invasive option that de-escalates the situation. Great teachers shrink issues instead of inflating them, and there are many ways to do this. When you notice Kathleen talking, the first thing you could do is use proximity. Instead of making the problem larger and bringing other students into the situation by saying, "Kathleen, you know better than to talk right now!" simply walk over toward her. You could have also chosen to kindly and genuinely ask her if she needs any help with the task. She may be asking the person next to her a question. You could also even have thanked someone near her for getting started right away, knowing that it could be an indirect way to remind Kathleen of your expectations. You could have simply ignored her. There is a chance that she wanted to say one thing really quickly and then she would be ready for class. As you can see, one teacher's response may not be exactly like another's, and that is okay. What is most important is that whatever the response, that it is the least-invasive option that de-escalates the situation.

Let's walk you through another scenario, but this time you are in the middle of teaching a whole class lesson. One of your students, Aiden, is 'messing around' in the back of the room. You use your proximity strategy, tap him on the back, and thank classmates near him for listening respectfully, but none of those have worked. A final "non-invasive" strategy you can use is including the struggling student in the lesson more. For example, you could call on him to answer a question, ask him to help you write information on the board, or even do a quick 30-second partner share and listen in on his conversation to hold him accountable. Having students engaged in a lesson is another form of behavior management, and the more effective and interesting your lesson structure is, the less behavior problems you will have.

With a student like this, or in any of the previous scenarios that have been used, if you felt like it was necessary, you could also take a minute or two to talk to the student outside of the classroom, or during a passing period or break, just to check up and see if anything else was going on. You could say something like, "Aiden, I noticed that you did not seem like yourself today. Is everything okay?" This conversation helps Aiden know that you did notice his misbehavior, but you are also genuinely concerned about his well-being. These quick conversations can be extremely critical when building relationships with your most struggling students. There is a chance that Aiden was still mad about something that happened at home that morning, or maybe he had extra energy that day. No matter what comes from this dialogue, you always want to go into it with genuine concern for the student. Assuming that the student did not behave with malicious intent gives you the freedom to use these quick conversations to build strong relationships.

This book is written by teachers for teachers, so we are not going to end this section pretending that proximity, ignoring, and engaging students fixes every single issue in the classroom. They don't, and we get it because we have our own complicated classrooms that we enter every day. Before we move on, however, we must make sure that you actually try these strategies before using ones from the next section. Sadly, many teachers complain about student misbehavior when they have not even tried these "go-to" techniques. If you sit behind your desk for the majority of a class period, have you really tried proximity? If you glare at a student for blurting out, was that really ignoring? If you had students read online documents and take notes on them for 60 minutes straight, were you really trying to engage your students? Again, we are teachers. We have used every good and bad classroom management technique just as you have. We challenge you, just as we challenge ourselves every day, to use this knowledge and make sure you try the trick that truly is the least-invasive option that also de-escalates the situation. Will it work perfectly every single time? No. Will you choose perfectly every time? Definitely not. But if you do not at least try them, how will you ever know if they work?

The Misbehavior Continues . . . Now What?

We are going to describe a scenario that may be all too familiar to some of you: You have that student, Kathleen, and she is very chatty during task one. You tried proximity; it didn't work. You complimented those around her; it didn't work. You even engaged her in the lesson more; it didn't work and honestly pretty much backfired because she ended up mumbling something under her breath that made students around her laugh. You're embarrassed because you are pretty sure she cracked a joke about you, and you are mad because Kathleen won't stop disrupting the class. She has either not gotten the hint (possible), or is knowingly defying you (likely), so what do you do?

Just as you responded the first times she misbehaved, you want to do something to make sure you are continuing to be consistent by reinforcing your expectations. Always remember to choose the least-invasive option that also de-escalates the situation. The problem is, however, that she has now been disruptive more than just once and part of the class has engaged in the situation. Learning time is now directly impacted, so "least-invasive" may potentially have to disrupt part of the learning environment. In this moment, effective classroom managers would respond in a variety of ways because teachers have different styles and ways of running their classrooms. We hope to give you a few options that we or our colleagues use in situations like this one. More importantly, however, is that we want you to see that every response has its pros and cons. Not one of them is perfect, and some will work better for younger students or older students. What's important is that, whichever response you choose, it be done correctly. Remember that an essential part of classroom management is managing yourself.

Eye Contact
What does this look like?
When you give eye contact, you can do it while you are teaching or you can make a brief pause to increase the impact. A simple moment of eye contact with a slight eyebrow raise lets the student know that you see what is going on and you are wanting and expecting it to stop.

Pros	*Cons*
The student knows immediately that you are aware of something that is going on. You do not have to say anything, which may allow you to continue the flow of what you are doing.	You are not directly telling the student to stop. The student may get defensive and respond.

Casual Redirection
What does this look like?
You could redirect Kathleen and the students around her by saying something like (potentially with a smile), "Okay, okay guys. Let's get back on track," and then quickly move on.

Pros	*Cons*
You are verbally acknowledging that a joke was made and that it disrupted the class, but you are showing students that it did not fluster you and you are ready to get back to work. Showing that you are not flustered can take the wind out of Kathleen's sail. Took up minimal instructional time.	You are not directly telling Kathleen to stop. If you do not have strong authority, it may not be a direct enough statement to get students to regroup.

Secret Note/Private Conversation
What does this look like?
You could give the student a blank, sealed envelope to deliver to a teacher directly across the hall. The teacher already knows that if a student from your class brings a blank, sealed envelope, all you need them to do is take the envelope, thank the student, and send them back. Then while they are delivering the note, you step out in the hallway and are now there to greet them. You thank them for delivering the note, and you get to have a private conversation and the student does not have their audience. Additionally it gives you a minute or two to gather yourself and make sure you handle the student in a more professional way than you would have if the student was in class with the other classmates watching.

Secret Note/Private Conversation	
Pros	*Cons*
The student is removed from the classroom in an inconspicuous way. You are able to have a private conversation with the student without letting the class know it will occur.	The student could potentially refuse to do the errand. It could backfire if the teacher says it in a mean or rude way. The student could also not return.

Private Conversation	
What does this look like? You could go to Kathleen or pull her aside and ask her if everything is okay. If everything is, then you can tell her that you love having her in class, but you also need her to be quiet at certain times so learning can take place.	
Pros	*Cons*
Directly telling her sends a signal to Kathleen's classmates about your ability to be consistent. It gives you a chance to see if there is anything deeper going on, or if she is just goofing around. It could potentially build the relationship if handled appropriately.	It could cause a negative reaction if she feels singled out or embarrassed.

Class Job	
What does this look like? You could come up with something for Kathleen to do that seems like it's helpful or important to you. 1. Be in charge of the projector remote. 2. Time me. 3. Fill up water bottle for me. 4. Run this to the office. 5. Collect everyone's homework. 6. Pass out these papers.	
Pros	*Cons*
It gets Kathleen out of the situation she currently is in. It may build the relationship because Kathleen may feel special. It potentially stops Kathleen's misbehavior by changing her train of thought.	It could give Kathleen a larger audience if she is extremely worked up. She could interpret it as a reinforcement of her misbehavior.

The Water Break	
What does this look like?	
You could respond by giving Kathleen an out if she really just needs a break from class. Say, "You seem _____ , want to go get a quick drink of water to see if that helps?" Insert tired, hungry, upset, sad, frustrated, etc.	
Pros	*Cons*
It potentially removes Kathleen from the classroom. It gives Kathleen a break if that is what she really needs. It does not cause a power struggle.	Kathleen may not need/want a drink or may just want an excuse to leave the classroom.

Let's Make a Deal	
What does this look like?	
You could make a deal with Kathleen that if she gets her assignment done during work time she could get some kind of benefit that you feel comfortable with. For example, she could work in a different location during the assignment or she could take a 3-minute break and work with a partner after that.	
Pros	*Cons*
It gives Kathleen some choice/power, which may be what she is needing in the moment. It could motivate her to not only stop disrupting the class, but also to get her work done.	If other students hear, they may also want to have the same deal. Kathleen may agree to take a break but not follow up on her end of the deal.

The New Seat	
What does this look like?	
You could move Kathleen to a new seat. Keeping your composure and confidence, you could simply state, "Kathleen I need you to move over here."	
Pros	*Cons*
It removes Kathleen from the situation. It shows her classmates that you do provide consequences when necessary.	She could refuse to move. She could cause a disruption on the way to the new seat. She could shut down and not do any work at her new seat.

Rely on Classroom Management System
What does this look like?
You could respond with a consequence based on your classroom management system, like by giving her a warning or taking away a point on a behavioral scale.

Rely on Classroom Management System	
Pros	Cons
It gives Kathleen immediate feedback about her behavior. It sends a signal to Kathleen's classmates about your ability to be consistent.	It could be handled inappropriately by the teacher and/or result in escalation. It could cause Kathleen to have an outburst and react in a stronger way than the original disruption.

Call Parents or Guardians	
What does this look like? You could respond by calling Kathleen's parents/guardians during a break in your day or after school, preferably without letting her know that you are doing so.	
Pros	Cons
It opens up communication lines with the home. It can improve Kathleen's behavior if parents/guardians implement consequences at home in response.	The parent/guardian doesn't believe you or doesn't feel that Kathleen did anything wrong. If positive contact wasn't made previously, your relationship with the parent/guardian may be hurt.

As mentioned previously, this is far from an exhaustive list of all of the ways that a teacher can respond to a student who is consistently misbehaving. We cannot recommend enough that you continue to ask colleagues for advice, look up tips online, and even think of ideas on your own. There is never one solution to a behavior management situation that will always work for you or all teachers, but the more you become aware of strategies you can use that are not invasive and de-escalate the situation, the better your classroom management abilities will get.

Somehow, It Gets Worse . . .

So let's say you try one (or more) of these strategies, but Kathleen has an outburst. An "I hate you and this school and this is so stupid" type of outburst. There may even be chairs or desks that are kicked or shoved (or worse . . .). What do you do? Once the situation escalates to this level, you must find an immediate and direct way to address the situation. At this point you have given Kathleen multiple chances to regroup and participate again, yet she still struggles. The learning environment has been entirely engulfed in this issue, and it's time to protect the learning and safety of the other students in the classroom.

Every teacher may respond in a different way, but you must respond with two things in mind. First, you must make sure you keep your composure throughout the entire scenario. Even though you are going to have to respond in a way that may feel severe, you still do not want to escalate the situation any more than it already is. Remember, you are the adult in the classroom so you must ensure the issue is the student's behavior and not make it become about the teacher's behavior. Second, make sure you respond in a way that will be most likely to get the student to calm down and do what you need her to do. Some students may respond when you say that they must go to the classroom next door or to the office, whereas others may need to be told to sit in the corner with their head down as you follow your school's protocol on this situation.

These are the situations that both new and seasoned teachers dread. Most of us go into teaching to make a difference, not to be yelled at or fear a student. With that said, there is good news. The more you refine your classroom management abilities, the less often situations like this occur. We are examples of this. When we started out, there were so many things we did wrong and that we wish we could change. As time goes on, however, we have been able to improve our management abilities so the majority of the time, students are successful learners. That does not mean that our classrooms are perfect (especially when we get "that" class!), but things are good enough that we truly love our jobs and our students.

Being Consistent Doesn't Mean Being Identical

After discussing consistency so much, we want to make sure that there is no misconception about what being consistent really looks like. Yes, it is all about reinforcing the behaviors that you want as well as your non-negotiables, but just because two different students break the same expectation or rule does not mean that you must treat both of those students the same. Let's say that you had two students blurt out while you were teaching a lesson. Sometimes, you may choose to respond to each student in the same way. For example, let's say you just implemented new stricter blurting-out policies in your class because it had become a problem. Thus, when the first student blurted out, you gave him or her the consequence you had in place, and you did the exact same thing when the second student blurted out as well.

With that said, there could be many times when you choose to respond in totally different ways. Sometimes your response depends on what happened previously during the lesson. For example, let's say the first student blurted out and you chose to ignore it by letting someone who raised his or her hand share instead. A few minutes later, another student blurted out. Since one student already blurted out and you ignored it, you should probably address it with the second student or the class may start to think that it is okay to blurt out. Other times, your response may depend on the needs of the student. If the first student who blurted out has an IEP for a diagnosis that may impact their in-class behavior, you will (and probably should) treat that student differently than the second one who has the capabilities to control himself or herself.

The key to consistency is not always about treating every student the same when misbehavior occurs. Instead, you should focus on trying your best to respond to each student in the way that will most likely improve his or her behavior in the future. For some, that means ignoring the behavior. For others, it means moving their seat the first time they blurt out. These are the moments when your expertise comes in. You know your students better than anyone else, so use that knowledge to do what is best for you, your classroom, and your kids.

Individual Case Study

Even with all of these "non-invasive" techniques in place, there is still a chance that you will have a few students who regularly struggle with misbehavior. For our first example, let's pretend you are having an issue with just one student, James. Even after using the multitude of strategies listed above, you are still consistently having the same problems with him: talking out, not completing work, messing around with classmates, etc. What do you do?

First, if the behaviors do not seem to distract other students, your flexibility in dealing with this is quite large. This shows that you have created the classroom climate that you want, and it is truly just this one student who is having issues. When it is just one student, you often have myriad choices and you can even be patient in choosing the best option. If it was a larger group of students having issues, you will have to seriously consider pressing the "reset button," which is something that will be discussed in chapter 6.

Additionally, when working with students like James, it is important to remember that making excuses will never ever help solve the problem. If you tell yourself that he has a tough home life, thus there is no way that you can get him to behave at school, you are actually doing him, the other students, and yourself a disservice. You must see the potential in him, because you are his teacher and you may be the only person in the school who actually believes in his ability to be a successful student.

We are going to walk you through the thought processes to take to figure out a way to help James. Before we begin, though, you must know that *we are assuming you and James have a good relationship*. If you do not, that needs to be a main focus as you problem-solve the situation. Remember it is very important to build a relationship before you need the relationship. Research identifies that teachers must begin to see classroom management as "an ongoing exercise in relationship building," especially for the most difficult students (Beaty-O'Ferrall, Green, & Hanna, 2010, p. 10). Remember, the success of your teaching relies on a foundation of great relationships with students.

Remember it is very important to build a relationship before you need the relationship.

Now, let's get back to the plan. To begin, you must ask yourself these three questions:

◆ When are most of the problems occurring?
◆ Am I doing something to perpetuate the problem?
◆ What can I do to help solve this problem?

The first thing you must be able to do is to reflect on James. When are most of the problems occurring? If you are an elementary teacher, you think about time of day—morning or afternoon? Before math or during writing? After lunch or after specials? If you are a secondary teacher, you will need to think in shorter time chunks. Right after the student walks in? Ten minutes into direct instruction? During group work? You may need to keep track on a notepad or device to document when the issues start. Finding this pattern can be critical because it will provide a basis for planning your behavior intervention plan.

Once you find this pattern, you then think about how you and/or your behavior may be negatively affecting the situation. If he is continually starting his class off in a non-productive way, think about how you may be perpetuating this. Has your seating chart placed him in a location that he cannot be successful in? Are your beginning-of-class structures tight enough for him to follow (no "down time," must work on bellringer, etc.)? Is he understanding the work that you are asking him to do? Remember to always have the mindset that you are the one who has the most influence on this student's behavior, so be honest with yourself about ways that you may be causing the misbehavior. As you go through this list remember to reflect to make sure you are doing these things consistently rather than intermittently.

After you think through these types of questions, the next step is to process through how you *can* help him. In working with students like James, there will never be an easy answer to your problems, so we recommend trying to find as many support systems for these types of students as possible. You may end up being able to come up with a solution for your classroom, and if that's the case, that's great! Many times, however, that will not be the situation. Every day students will come to school with issues, some simple and some earth-shatteringly painful. When everything you have tried still does not seem to help, we recommend reaching out to the following resources if possible: other teachers, administrators, counselors, behavior specialists, special education teachers, intervention specialists/committees, psychologists, and student advocates.

Sometimes this will lead to fruitful solutions, while other times the year will end and you will be unsure if you did anything that actually even helped. That's okay. We have lived through all sorts of outcomes with students like James, so we understand. What's important to remember is that you always try to find a solution. Sometimes the solution will help James be successful in school, whereas other times the best solution is one that protects your class's learning time. Few things in education are simple, so even though we want you to try everything you can to improve the child's situation, don't beat yourself up if your hard work doesn't make everything perfect.

Tweak

As we have mentioned previously, we have found that most teachers who feel that they struggle with classroom management say that consistency is the part of the house metaphor that is causing the most issues. Some teachers feel that they are not consistent enough. Some are actually proud of their consistency, but they can tell that it is hurting their relationships with students. We will admit that there is no way to get this right all the time. There is good reason that teachers say it is the aspect of management that they struggle with the most because it really is the hardest to get right! We are going to walk you through a few common problems that teachers face with consistency and things you can do to fix them. Although we hope you can find a solution to your issue, we also want to let you know that improving consistency only comes with purposeful practice over time. It will not be an easy fix, but it will be one that is worth it.

Problem 1: You Are Struggling to Give Consequences Because You Are Scared That Students Will Stop Liking You

Some teachers, especially those who are newer to the profession, may struggle to consistently provide consequences because they are afraid that it will cause the students not to like them. We definitely understand that, because if all of your classes hated you, the fun in teaching would be sucked away. With that said, we want to reassure you that the large majority of students can and will still like you even if you need to give them consequences. In the moment, they may lash out or say hurtful things, but as long as you follow these guidelines, your relationships should come out untarnished or even stronger.

1. Keep your cool. When you give a consequence, always make sure you are staying as calm as possible. If you start yelling and lash out, the student could potentially lose trust in you. Be confident and stern when necessary (because sometimes that is what is needed), but don't become mean about it. Even though the student may be mad in the moment, if you are respectful then they will maintain their respect for you.

2. Explain why you gave a consequence. If you give reasoning as to why you chose the consequence that you did, there is a better chance that the student will be more understanding of your response to their behavior. For example, if a student was struggling to pay attention during class because they were continually talking to the person next to them, you could explain that beginning the next class they will start out in a different seat away from their friend because it will help them be more successful and get more work completed. Although this is not fool-proof, we have found that many students eventually understand what they did wrong and why the consequence matches their behavior. Additionally, even if this student does not accept the result, other students will be more supportive of the teacher because of the logical consequence.

3. Let the student choose the consequence. To help build student ownership of a misbehavior, Jim Fay and David Funk (1995) recommend that teachers give students a say in what their consequences should be in *Teaching With Love and Logic*. After a student misbehaves, you could explain 2–3 consequences that you feel comfortable with and let the student choose the one that he or she prefers. Eventually, if you do this consistently enough, students may even be able to come up with logical consequences on their own without choices.

4. Make your consequences fair. When giving a consequence, try to make sure it matches the misbehavior. Teachers who

give consequences that are too weak (like a teacher who ignores the situation when a student is getting bullied) or too harsh (like giving a student an office referral for forgetting a pencil) will struggle to maintain authority and respect. If there is a chance that the consequences you have been giving are too far on one of the ends of the spectrum, think through whether they are fair.

5.   Remember that you are the teacher. When you come to school every day, you should not be showing up to become your students' best friend forever. Yes, you want them to feel comfortable sharing stories and laughs with you, but at the end of the day, you are their teacher. You are there to guide and direct them to becoming adults themselves, which means that sometimes they may not like a decision you have to make. As you all know, students will do and say a lot of things to try and get out of doing work! If you become too concerned with students liking you, there is a chance that any semblance of a classroom management system you had will quickly crumble (if it hasn't already). Just remember that even the best teachers have students who don't always love them, and that's okay. What's important is that every day you remember that every decision you make has their best interest at heart.

Problem 2: You Are So Consistent That You May Actually Be Giving Consequences in an Unfair Way

Some teachers may actually be skilled at being consistent, but sometimes that skill can backfire if you don't realize that some students need to be treated differently from others. Remember that consistency means that you are making a purposeful decision to respond (or not respond) to each misbehavior. That purposeful decision may not look the same for each student. In some situations it is entirely okay to give students the same consequences. For example, maybe your cell phone policy starts with a warning when a student brings it out at an inappropriate time, then if it is pulled out again when it should not be, you make a phone call home. This could be a fair consequence for all students, as long as there isn't someone who needs their device according to an IEP or 504 plan.

In other situations, however, giving different consequences may serve you and your students better. For example, maybe you have two students who talk in class one day. One student generally has a talking problem in class every day, whereas the other student is incredibly shy and it feels like a miracle when he actually says something during the class discussion. When each student talks, it probably wouldn't be fair to give them both the exact same consequence. The student who has the perpetual issue should be given a clear and direct consequence, whether it is a private conversation, warning, moving a seat, etc. The other student, however, is not a persistent talker, so there is a chance that simply ignoring it will fix the issue because it may not actually be an issue.

We are obviously not in your current classroom and do not know your student dynamics, so this exact example may not apply to you. We hope, however, that it pushes you to think about how you are being consistent in your classroom, and if you are giving yourself some flexibility within the consistency.

Problem 3: You Are Struggling to Keep Track of Consequences You Give, and It All Feels Too Hard to Manage

Some teachers find themselves in situations where they are trying to keep track of too many behaviors, and eventually they feel like they can't be consistent with *any* part of their management system. Although sometimes this may be unavoidable because of required behavior plans for certain students, if you feel this way about managing the majority of your students, there is a good chance that you are trying to do too much at once. Over time, teachers can build skills that allow them to remember and keep track of a multitude of misbehaviors, but if you can tell that this is not where you currently find yourself, we recommend a few things.

1. Focus on a few non-negotiables. Think of 1–3 things that you *have* to have your students do to keep your classroom running smoothly and focus on those. As teachers, we are not required to make our students behave like perfect

angels 100 percent of the time. We do, however, need students to follow a few rules for learning to consistently occur in the classroom. For some teachers, one non-negotiable may be that students must follow directions the first time. For other teachers, it may be needing students not to blurt out during direction instruction. No matter what your non-negotiables are, identify them and focus on making sure students follow those and not other less-important expectations. Over time, there is a good chance that you will find that your capacity for managing more than you could before will increase.

2. Find a way to keep track of misbehaviors. Even if you have your non-negotiables identified, it can sometimes be hard to keep track of which students did what and when it occurred. We recommend that you find some way to keep track of the misbehaviors to make sure you can follow through with necessary consequences. Teachers can keep track of these with online tools (e.g., Google Doc, ClassDojo, Microsoft Excel), physical representations (clip charts, card systems), or using hand-written notes (e.g., Post-its, class list on a clipboard, planner). You will most likely need to try out a few strategies until you find one that works for you. The good news, however, is that once you find one that fits your style, it will become easier and easier to use as it becomes a part of your normal routine. Finding this sweet spot enables you to be much more consistent.

✓ What You Can Do Tomorrow

1. **Have a Laser Focus.** Think about one expectation that students have not been following that has been really hurting your management abilities and classroom culture. Choose to focus on that over the next days and/or weeks. Decide how you will hold students accountable for their misbehavior and follow through with your decisions and make this a focus of your consistency for the remainder of your school year.

2. **Use Tricks Less Frequently.** Remember that the best teachers do not have to use 1,342 tricks in one day. Instead, they work to prevent as many misbehaviors as possible, so the ones that do inevitably occur will be manageable. Think of one part of your day where you deplete your bag of tricks quickly. Is there something you could tweak about a procedure, expectation, lesson, etc. that could prevent any potential misbehaviors? Even if you have to use 10 less tricks thanks to that small adjustment, that's still 10 less tricks!

3. **Choose Tricks Wisely.** Reflect on situations that recently occurred where you feel like you chose the wrong trick for that situation. Think about which trick you could have chosen that would have been better. Maybe you needed to diffuse the situation instead of escalating it. Maybe you needed to be more firm and confident in your response instead of ignoring the occurrence. No matter what trick you used before, decide which one you will use instead next time and try it out.

4. **"That" Student.** You may have one or two students in particular who are making your year incredibly stressful and difficult. If you have not done this already, please reach out to other people in your building or district to see if there are resources that can be offered to you or your student. You do not have to survive on an island. Even though all changes have to start with you, they do not always have to end with you.

6

The Reset—Your Last Resort

Personal Reflection—Katherine

It was October my first year of teaching. It was a Thursday, in fact, during my 4th hour class. This day and that class are forever ingrained in my mind. I could not tell you what I was attempting to teach that day, but I can tell you that not a whole lot of teaching occurred. Things in my classes had generally been going downhill, and this day was where I hit rock bottom. The kids walked into class, the bell rang, and literally not one of them was in a seat or even pretending like it was time to move toward their seats. I remember standing at the front of the room asking kids to have a seat. They were so loud that only a couple of students heard me. I started working my way around the room to the various groups of students and tried to break them up and get them seated. I was starting class off completely frustrated, but this had been my routine for a few weeks now. There seemed to be no other way to do it. This whole 'asking kids to take a seat' process was always a highly stressful 3–5 minutes for me, but I always felt some relief when I was able to begin the lesson.

On this particular day, I remember explaining the first example for my lesson when a student yelled out, "Can I go to the bathroom!?" I had set the precedent at the beginning of the year that we had to be done with the note-taking part of the lesson before students could use the bathroom, so after the student yelled out I reminded him that he had to wait until notes were done. Eye rolling and sighs ensued on the part of the student. Frustration and increased blood pressure ensued on the side of the teacher, but we persisted. I had made it to example 2. I remember scanning the class to make sure students were ready for the next example when I noticed that four students were at the pencil sharpener. Frustrated but determined, I ignored them and powered through my second example.

All four students were still at the pencil sharpener when I completed the example, so I made my way back there to see what was going on. When I arrived, I realized that only one actually had to sharpen his pencil and he had already done that, yet he chose to stay back there with his friends anyway. The other three students were pretending to sharpen pencils, even though I saw two of them holding mechanical pencils and one holding *a pen*. They all just wanted to avoid me and my lesson. I still remember how heartbreaking that feeling was to this day. I was frustrated and crushed all at the same time.

After some coaxing, I convinced them to get back to their seats so I could move onto example 3. I was asking questions about the example, desperately attempting to re-engage my class, but every question got a shouted response of "21!" from students scattered around the room. Although I was ignoring the outburst, on the inside I was fuming. Students were randomly getting up to throw scraps of paper away. From what? I had no idea. They were causing disruptions with one student getting pushed while walking back from the trash can. I looked around the room and realized that by the end of example 3 I had lost my class. The entire class.

I quit trying to get students to take notes. I refused to continue this fight, so I passed out the worksheet and asked the students to get started. As if orchestrated, everyone instantly got up and moved around the room to work with friends. During this chaos, I heard what felt like 1 million complaints about how they did not understand how to do this assignment. The complaints did not stop. All I got for the next 10 minutes were basic questions about the lesson because they had not paid attention during notes. Complaint after complaint after complaint accosted me. I realized after those 10 minutes that hardly anyone had even attempted anything on their class-work. All this tension had built up and I lost it. I blew up.

"Enough! Everyone, back to your seats! I do not want to hear another word!" I remember distinctly that there were 7 minutes left in the hour. I made everyone put their heads down and told them if they made a sound they were getting sent to the office. I was done. My heart was racing during the longest 7 minutes of my life. I remember praying that no one made a sound because I was not about to send a kid to the office over this. How am I going to defend my actions to my principal? All I could do was picture how the conversation would go . . . "So I yelled at my entire class and made them sit at their desks with their heads down and threatened to send them to the office if they made a sound and . . . he made a sound."

Thank goodness no one made a sound. The bell rang, and as the last kid left my room, tears started streaming down my face. Who was this teacher that I had become? How embarrassing is it that I cannot get through three examples with my class without 1,000 distractions? Who am I supposed to ask to help me? I should know how to do this. But I did not. This situation was not fixable by tweaking a couple things, this was a culture and climate issue. The only thing I had going for me were the relationships I had with my kids. The fact that they really did not make a sound after that threat showed I still had some respect and authority. But other than that, I had nothing. I needed a last resort. I needed to reset my entire classroom.

How-to and Application

As mentioned in chapter 1, the "Reset" is when your classroom management is in such a state of disarray that nearly everything about it must change: your relationships, expectations, rules, procedures, consistency, and classroom culture. Since so much will be changing, you must not rush a reset. You should not decide impulsively in the middle of class to change everything. This is because you can generally only have an effective reset once per year, maybe twice if you are lucky. As we will explain further in the next sections, you must think through everything that needs to be changed, and make a plan on how this will be communicated with students.

We call the reset the "last resort" in classroom management because of the seriousness of the tool. Before we get into the reasons for a reset or how to implement one, we want to make one thing crystal clear: Having to use a reset because all else has failed does not make you a failure of a teacher. It makes you a teacher that is willing to fight. Not only are you fighting for yourself when you implement a reset, but you are fighting for your students. You want to be able to teach, but more importantly you want your students to be able to learn. That being said, if you have hit a point in your school year where you are feeling defeated, ashamed, frustrated, or sad—keep fighting. It's not over, you do not have to be defeated, you can still succeed.

> Having to use a reset because all else has failed does not make you a failure of a teacher.

In the spirit of full transparency, my sister and I are such huge proponents of the reset because we have both had to do it. We have both felt defeated. We have both felt ashamed. We have both felt like failures. However, we fought. We fought for our classrooms, our own personal sanity, and for our students every single day.

I. Identify the Issues

To get your reset planned out, the first thing you have to do is identify the issues. What is happening in your classroom that is not working for you? If you are elementary, you need to figure out if the entire day is a disaster or if it is just the afternoon? Are students focused and on-task during free-write time but bouncing off the walls during math circles? You need to sit down and think through your entire day to identify the exact times and places where you can no longer teach and your students can no longer learn. At the secondary level, you need to decide whether or not every class/hour/period is struggling or if it is just one or two of them. Maybe your honors classes are always on task, but your regular classes cannot effectively function under the current rules and procedures. We would even recommend taking a day of teaching to jot down notes of when the rough patches start to show up. Taking the time to self-reflect on a day is really going to help you decipher just how big the issue is. Try to be as specific as you can. If there is someone in the building you trust, have them come in and observe you, but be specific about what you want them to look for. For example, when exactly do my kids get off-task? What am I doing? Which kids get off-task? Where am I in the room? The goal of this observation should specifically be for data. You are not asking for an opinion about your teaching style or methods to correct the behavior, you just need an accurate picture of when things begin to start their downward spiral.

Once you have pinpointed the times that you can no longer teach and your students can no longer learn, you then have to figure out why. Identify the behaviors you do not like and think through why they are happening. You may come up with a list of things that are not going well, or just one thing that needs major adjustment. For example, let's say that you feel your whole first hour is out of control. However, after serious reflection and maybe even an observation by another trusted educator, you realize that the majority of the issues actually stem from one thing: students getting out of their seat at any time during the lesson. You did not realize that students getting out of their seats whenever they wanted was going to be an issue, but now they are distracting the entire class by dunking their trash into the trashcan 14 times each hour. That is the expectation change that needs to be made and then implemented with consistency. In an elementary classroom, you might realize that the majority of the day actually goes really well. However, after recess is math time, and the battle of getting students to calm down and engage in the lesson or activity is exhausting. Math seems to be everyone's least favorite time of day and you cannot continue the year like this. You realize this is the area of the day you need to focus on when resetting.

II. Classify the Issues

At this point you should know where your issues lie, whether they are with one class, one "chunk" of your day, or the entire day, beginning to end. Once this has been done, you now need to determine which issues stem from ineffective lessons, which are foundational (relationships), which are structural (high and clear expectations), and which are due to a lack of maintenance (consistency). This step of the reset is key to your success, so please be sure to be entirely honest with yourself about what is going on in your classroom. Do not feel any shame for having to admit what is wrong. Believe us, we have *all* been there, whether it was our first year or a year with a particularly tough group of students. Be real about what needs to change, and you will set yourself up for a better tomorrow.

The first issues you need to identify are ones that pertain to your lessons. Are your lessons organized? Are you ready to have students engaged in the material from the moment they walk into the classroom? Is the content accessible to all of your students? Are you clearly identifying and explaining the standards that students are to know? Are you avoiding giving students "down time"? When reflecting on your lessons, we recommend either having someone you trust observe you or recording yourself to see where the major issues lie. You can also observe master teachers who are known to be highly organized and structured, or even ask your students themselves in person or in a survey to see if they can clarify specific issues in the lesson structure.

Foundational issues are the ones that pertain to your relationships with students. Do you feel like you have good relationships, but student behavior says otherwise? Or do you have good relationships, but that may be due to the fact that you have forgotten that you are the teacher more than the friend? Maybe you really do have good relationships, but it's everything else in your classroom that isn't working? We would recommend going back to the "Tweak" section in chapter 3 to see if any of the scenarios we described seem to reflect what is occurring in your classroom.

Structural issues pertain to your classroom rules, procedures, and expectations. Do you have classroom rules that are reasonable and maintainable? Do you have understandable procedures for everything from sharpening a pencil to storing technology? Do you have clear expectations for behaviors that push students to be the best they can be while in your classroom? Again, either having someone observe you in your classroom and/or observing a master teacher could help you identify major issues that you have pertaining to expectations of your students. We would recommend scanning through the different parts of chapter 4 and either highlight or note the areas that you know need to be improved.

The final category of issues pertains to lack of maintenance. From our experience, most teachers we have worked with identify this category being the one that they struggle the most with. Teachers who struggle with this category are those that typically have expectations that may even be high and clear, but they struggle to hold students accountable to them. For example, maybe every single student could explain what he or she needed to do when they first walked in the classroom, but they never seem to actually do it. Or maybe you have such good relationships with students that you feel hesitant to actually redirect them when misbehaviors are occurring. You may even be holding students accountable, but in unfair or unnecessarily harsh ways. If you feel any of these may be your situation, we recommend going back to chapter 5 and seeing if any of the tweaks resonate with you.

III. Find Solutions for the Issues

Once you have done the tough but important work in classifying your issues, you now must work to find solutions to the issues that you have identified. A key part of this step is to make sure that you do not use excuses to prevent you from finding solutions. As teachers, we truly understand that classroom management issues can seem hopeless. There are *definitely* some classes or groups of students that are more challenging than others, so we are not asking you to find a way to turn your students into perfect robot learners. Instead, we want you to find a solution so *you* stay sane and the students are able to learn. You are so important to the teaching community, and if we all gave up after an impossible day, there would be none of us left. So as you are working to find solutions to your issues, we want you to focus on the ways that issues can possibly be fixed because that is what will give you and your students hope for tomorrow. Sometimes hope is all we need to make the changes that are necessary.

So where do you look to find solutions? We wish we could list all of the necessary solutions in this book so you wouldn't have to spend too much time on this, but sadly the world of working with kids and young adults does not work that way. Instead, we hope we can give you ideas that our colleagues and we have used when finding solutions is necessary.

1. **Other teachers.** Many times, colleagues at your school have found solutions to issues you are facing on a day-to-day basis, so using them as resources can sometimes be your best bet. They share the same building as you and understand your school culture, climate, clientele, and general district expectations, so it can make your conversations potentially easier and more understandable. What if you do not have a teacher at your school that you feel comfortable connecting with, though? If this is your situation, we highly recommend connecting with those outside of your school via social media (which we will explain next), conferences, or even through teacher-friends. Sometimes getting an outside perspective can help you see issues and situations through a different lens, and can bring ideas to you that you may have never come across before.

2. **Social media.** Connecting with other teachers on social media can be another great way to find solutions to the issues you face while preparing for a reset. Twitter, Facebook, Instagram, and others provide easy ways for you to access new information and to connect with those who may not be geographically close to you. One warning we do want to make is that you should not compare your own classroom experience to others that may seem "perfect." One of the drawbacks of social media is that people

generally do not post pictures about their worst days, so it tends to be a highly filtered version of reality. Make sure that you use social media to the benefit of yourself and your kids, not as a comparison tool.

3. **Administration or instructional coach.** Another person-to-person strategy you could use is either administration or your building's or district's instructional coach. Invite them into your classroom and tell them specific things you are wanting feedback on. You could also set up a one-on-one conversation with them to explain how things are going in your classroom and what you need help with. Many times, these school leaders have experience and/or training in helping teachers improve their craft.

4. **Books and publications.** For those of us who prefer more self-reflective learning, books and articles are great go-tos for finding solutions. A multitude of high-quality books about management and instructional practices have been published over many decades, with a great combination of research-based and practical strategies that teachers can use to improve their classrooms. We would recommend doing some research before you choose to buy a certain book just so you can make sure it will provide you with the specific guidance you are hoping for.

5. **Educational blogs and articles.** Although we saved this one for last, we have found that educational blogs can be one of the best resources for teachers who are wanting advice on specific classroom management techniques and structures. Since blogs are updated in real-time, you can find information on all of the latest strategies that teachers use to manage their classrooms. You can even search for specific tips, like "how to make sure classroom expectations are clear" or "how to choose fair consequences in the classroom." These can really help when you are trying to refine the solutions you are hoping to use in your classroom.

IV. Hold Students Accountable

Before we jump in on how to officially do the reset, we understand that most teachers in this situation start to think about "What ifs?" What if the student blurts out while I am talking? What if they argue with me as I am explaining the new expectations? What if this all backfires? Doing a reset is scary, not only because it is new for you and your students, but also because these things will *most likely* happen. If students are used to being in a classroom with little structure, they will quite possibly resist when new expectations are put in place.

The main recommendation that we can make for you before you jump in is to have a plan for when these things happen. Do not go in assuming that you will give your new classroom structure and everything will be hunky-dorey. Instead, plan for students blurting out. Plan for students resisting. Plan for students asking questions. How you respond will be important in setting the tone for the reset, so we want you to make sure that you have thought through how you will handle student misbehavior on day 1 of the reset and day 101 of the reset. You have to have a classroom management plan in place. So once again, do not be in a rush to make this reset happen. You want to have thought through all possible scenarios as you may only have one chance to reset.

So let's say you are explaining the reset to your class, and a student blurts out. What would you do? Well, we want you to do whatever you will do when a student blurts out during a lesson on a normal day near the beginning of the year. Remember, in these situations you are wanting to make sure that students know your expectations clearly. Maybe you ignore the first student who blurts out, or maybe you tell the student that you will be happy to answer his or her question when a hand is raised. No matter your response, we just want to make sure it is purposeful and has been thought through. If you are reading this and realize that you need to spend more time thinking about the "what ifs," please go back to chapter 5 and read through the sections that describe how to handle student misbehavior. Although the planning will get you ready for the reset, your ability to consistently hold students to high expectations when you begin is what will make it successful.

The Reset

You have identified your issues, classified them, and even found potential solutions you are ready to try. Maybe you have new rules for your students or new procedures you want to implement. You might even have a new standard for yourself on how to hold students accountable when rules are broken. You were patient with yourself as you took the appropriate amount of time to plan for your reset, and now you are ready to push the "reset button."

This is a big moment. This is your chance to remake your classroom back into what you hoped it could be. To make sure it goes as well as possible, we recommend doing the reset at a natural break in the school year, maybe after a long weekend or a holiday. With that said, we also understand that sometimes the reset needs to happen *now*. That is fine, as long as you have thought through it extensively and fully planned it before you jump in. No matter the rules, procedures, or expectations you introduce, they must be upheld by *you* through your actions.

It is a Monday. You spent the entire weekend planning your new classroom. You re-read certain sections of the book with your more experienced lens. You have explicitly written out the new expectations, procedures, and/or rules. You have thought through how you are going to uphold them. You know you are going to compliment students doing things the way you want them done. You know you are going to redirect those not following the new expectations immediately. You are ready to introduce this to your students.

Right when students walk in on the first day of the reset, you start the class off by introducing and explaining the changes you are making. Here is an example of the language you can use. "I was thinking this weekend about our class and decided it was time to improve our learning environment. I have come up with some new procedures and am so excited to introduce them. I want to make it so we can all work together to ensure everyone has the best learning experience they can. So here is what I came up with . . . " At this point you would introduce the changes.

What is important about the language above is that you are positive while also exuding unwavering confidence about the future. Before the reset, you may have been really frustrated with your students' behavior. However, there is no need to even mention their previous behavior or place any blame on them. Do not bring up the past because they will latch on to it and refuse to move forward with you. Remember that you all are a team and you want to work with them to be successful. Barely address the past and quickly move to fixing things for a better future.

Now that you have introduced the reset to students you have to maintain it. To maintain the reset, you have to uphold the new procedures and expectations. Stay strong no matter what. The students will try to resort back to their old behavior or ways of doing things. You have to make sure you address each situation, redirect quickly, and have consequences in place if need be. Consistency is key.

If you can uphold your reset for a solid two to three weeks, you will be amazed how much your classroom environment will change. You may have to be more stern and serious than you prefer to be, but you have to sacrifice for a while so learning can take place in your classroom. Remember, it is much easier to loosen expectations than to make them tighter, so stick to what you have planned and what you know is needed to have a positive classroom culture. Over time, students will adjust and everyone will benefit from it.

The following are a few examples on how we have worked to uphold the new expectations when we ourselves have done a reset. Obviously, everyone's reset will be different, but we wanted to share some advice for common trends we have found in classroom management situations.

Example 1: The day of the reset you say that students will no longer shout out answers during the lesson. If they have something to say, whether it be an answer or a question, they must raise their hand. After explaining the reset you start your lesson. Five minutes in, you pose a question and Quinn shouts out the correct answer. Knowing your students, you realize that you MUST address this or else other students will start doing it as well. So you respond, "Quinn, I love that you knew the correct answer, but this does not follow our new expectations, can you try that again?" You decided to force her to raise her hand so you could call on her and thank her for raising her hand and giving the correct answer. Although this feels silly, you really want a change to occur and you know that things have to get uncomfortable before anything can get better.

Example 2: Let's say a few minutes later you pose a question, 15 students raise their hands, but you still have three students shout out answers. You know that students are aware of the expectation, so you choose to praise and ignore. "George, thank you so much for raising your hand! What are your thoughts?" This way, the conversation and your confidence was not rattled. Additionally, you were able to bring positivity into the classroom.

Example 3: By the end of the lesson most students have caught on, but you realize that Anthony is still shouting out. You know that this must be dealt with before you teach your next lesson. During a brief moment between classes or during a transition (like when you drop students off at lunch or walk them to a related arts class), you walk up to him, lean down, and say, "Anthony, I noticed you were struggling to follow our new procedure. I know raising your hand can be hard, but when you do that you are interrupting other students' thinking processes. Tomorrow I will give you one warning, but if you shout out an answer twice in the lesson you are going to have to go to a buddy room. Do you have any questions about this?" You know removing Anthony out of the learning environment for not raising his hand seems extreme, but this is a change that must be made so you can teach and the students can learn. You still vividly remember when your classroom was out of control and you know that you have to be very consistent about these changes so students take them seriously. The next day before class starts you are planning to have a quick conversation with Anthony before he enters the room. You know that reminding him of your expectations will be the best way to help set him up for success in your classroom after the reset.

*   *   *

As a final thought, you must remember that you can only push the "reset button" once (maybe twice) a year. It is a powerful tool, but each time you use it, it becomes less and less significant. If you "reset" once and do it well, students will take it seriously. If you "reset" a second time, students are going to wonder why you keep changing it up, and they may start finding a pattern. The third time you openly "reset," it will most likely turn into a joke. We highly recommend that you push the "reset button" when necessary, just make sure it is always done with careful thought and preparation because it is your last resort.

Epilogue: Conclusion → Your Tomorrow

We are honored you chose to read this book and your students are fortunate that you chose to teach. Teaching is the most rewarding, challenging, and exhausting profession that there is. Some people compare it to being a brain surgeon in difficulty. This would be true if the brain surgeon was in the operating room with 24 other patients and none of them were sedated, and most likely no scrub nurse and a 14-year-old scalpel.

You chose to teach for a reason—to make a difference. And you do. But sometimes we may feel overwhelmed. We may at times feel that our impact is more minimal than we imagined. Sometimes we may be tempted to throw our hands in the air and surrender. This is natural. There are many reasons for our frustration. Continually changing state mandates, increasing demands from the district office, lack of parental support at school or at home, too few resources, etc. Coming up with difficulties is fairly easy. However, the list of benefits is also substantial—impact students' lives, make a difference every day, have a job that truly matters, leave a legacy that lives forever, and on and on. But we know that what really determines success in a school is founded in what each teacher does in their own classroom. That is where we get to create, care, and share joy.

Remember, to build and maintain a house you need three main things: a strong foundation, the actual house structure, and regular upkeep. When thinking about managing a classroom, you also need three things: strong relationships, high and clear expectations, and consistency. Although there will be areas of strength for us all, we need to always remember that having a well-run classroom requires all three. Some days you may need to adjust your relationships, other days you may need to tweak your consistency. Some days your lessons may need to be improved, other days your expectations may need to be clearer. No matter what needs to be tweaked, always remember how interconnected they each are.

Strong relationships, high and clear expectations, and consistency are the blueprint to being the teacher that your students need and deserve. You have the tools. This book was not designed to be a prefab approach to classroom management. Instead, think of this as a blueprint. You are the architect, construction head, and the interior decorator. With your caring approach and well-designed plans, you work everyday to make your classroom into a home for learning. Whether it is your 1st year or your 21st year, whether you are looking for a starter home, a fixer-upper, or adding an additional room in a luxury neighborhood, we hope that this book can help you build your house, from the ground up.

References

Bain, H. P., & Jacobs, R. (1990, September). The case for smaller classes and better teachers. *Streamlined Seminar—National Association of Elementary School Principals, 9*(1).

Beaty-O'Ferrall, M. E., Green, A., & Hanna, F. (2010, March). Classroom management strategies for difficult students: Promoting change through relationships. *Middle School Journal, 41*(4), 4–11.

Boostrom, R. (1991). The nature and function of classroom rules. *Curriculum Inquiry, 21*(2), 193–216.

Brophy, J. E. (1996). *Teaching problem students.* New York, NY: Guilford Press.

Bunce, D. M., Flens, E. A., & Neiles, K. Y. (2010). How long can students pay attention in class? A study of student attention decline using clickers. *Journal of Chemical Education, 87*(12), 1438–1443.

Chang, M.-L. (2009). An appraisal perspective of teacher burnout: Examining the emotional work of teachers. *Educational Psychology Review, 21*, 193–218.

Cornelius-White, J. (2007). Learner-centered teacher-student relationships are effective: A meta-analysis. *Review of Educational Research, 77*(1), 113–143.

Emmer, E. T., Evertson, C. M., & Anderson, L. M. (1980). Effective classroom management at the beginning of the school year. *The Elementary School Journal, 80*(5), 219–231.

Emmer, E. T., & Saborine, E. J. (2015). *Handbook of classroom management* (2nd ed.). New York: Routledge Publishing Company.

Fay, J., & Funk, D. (1995). *Teaching with love and logic.* Golden, CO: The Love and Logic Press.

Friedman, I. A. (2006). Classroom management and teacher stress and burnout. In C. M. Evertson & C. S. Weinstein (Eds.), *Handbook of classroom management: Research, practice, and contemporary issues* (925–944). Mahwah, NJ: Erlbaum.

Hamre, B. K., & Pianta, R. C. (2006). Chapter 5: Student-teacher relationships. In G. G. Bear & K. M. Minke (Eds.), *Children's needs III: Development, prevention and intervention* (3rd ed.). Bethesda, MD: National Association of School Psychologists.

Jones, F. (2013). *Tools for teaching: Discipline, instruction, motivation* (3rd ed.). Santa Cruz, CA: Fredric H. Jones & Associates Inc.

Klassen, R. M., & Chiu, M. M. (2010). Effects on teachers' self-efficacy and job satisfaction: Teacher gender, years of experience, and job stress. *Journal of Educational Psychology, 102*(3), 741–756.

Lacourse, F. (2011). An element of practical knowledge in education: Professional routines. *McGill Journal of Education, 46*(1), 73–90.

Lemov, D. (2010). *Teach like a champion: 49 Techniques that put students on the path to college.* San Francisco, CA: Jossey-Bass.

Lester, R. R., Allanson, P. B., & Notar, C. E. (2017). Routines are the foundation of classroom management. *Education, 137*(4), 398–410.

Marzano, R. J. (2011, March). Relating to students: It's what you do that counts. *Educational Leadership*, 82–83.

Marzano, R. J. (2007). *The art and science of teaching.* Alexandria, VA: ASCD.

Marzano, R. J., Gaddy, B. B., Foseid, M. C., Foseid, M. P., & Marzano, J. S. (2005). *A handbook for classroom management that works.* Alexandria, VA: Association for Supervision and Curriculum Development.

Peart, N. A., & Campbell, F. A. (1999). At-risk students' perceptions of teacher effectiveness. *Journal for a Just and Caring Education, 5*(3), 269–284.

Polk, J. A. (2006). Traits of effective teachers. *Arts Education Policy Review, 107*(4), 23–29.

Roorda, D. L., Koomen, H. M. Y., Spilt, J. L., & Oort, F. J. (2011). The influence of affective teacher–student relationships on students' school engagement and achievement: A meta-analytic approach. *Review of Educational Research, 81*(4), 493–529.

Rosenshine, B. (2012). Principles of instruction: Research-based strategies that all teachers should know. *American Educator, 36*(1), 12–19.

Savage, T. V., & Savage, M. K. (2009). *Successful classroom management and discipline: Teaching self control and responsibility* (3rd ed.). Thousand Oaks, CA: SAGE Publications.

Stronge, J. H. (2007). *Qualities of effective teachers* (2nd ed.). Alexandria, VA: Association for Supervision and Curriculum Development.

Stronge, J. H., Tucker, P. D., & Ward, T. J. (2003). *Teacher effectiveness and student learning: What do good teachers do?* Paper presented at the American Educational Research Association Annual Meeting, Chicago, IL.

Taylor, B. M., Pearson, P. D., Clark, K. F., & Walpole, S. (1999). Center for the improvement of early reading achievement: Effective schools/accomplished teachers. *The Reading Teacher, 53*(2), 156–159.

Titsworth, S., Mazer, J. P., Goodboy, A. K., Bolkan, S., & Myers, S. A. (2015). Two meta-analyses exploring the relationship between teacher clarity and student learning. *Communication Education, 64*(4), 385–418.

Wasicisko, M. M., & Ross, S. M. (1994, May/June). *How to create discipline problems: The clearing house.* Washington, DC: Heldref Publications. (In K. Ryan & J. M. Cooper (Eds.), *Kaleidoscope: Contemporary and classic readings in education* [12th ed.]. Belmont, CA: Wadsworth Cengage Learning [2010]).

Whitaker, T. (2012). *What great teachers do differently* (2nd ed.). New York, NY: Routledge.

Whitaker, T., & Fiore, D. (2016). *Dealing with difficult parents* (2nd ed.). New York, NY: Routledge.

Whitaker, T., Whitaker, M., & Whitaker, K. (2016). *Your first year: How to survive and thrive as a new teacher.* New York, NY: Routledge.